HARBOR CITY CHRONICLES

The People & Culture

Apostle Islands · Bayfield Peninsula · Chequamegon Bay

Robert J. Nelson

Historien er Livets Laerer - Norske - *History is Life's Teacher*

A Journalistic History with Photos
Volume One

Robert J. Nelson

HARBOR CITY CHRONICLES
THE PEOPLE & CULTURE
VOLUME ONE

ROBERT J NELSON

Printed in the United States of Americirca

Published by
Blue Box Press
An Inprint of Blue Box Design LLC
PO Box 1333
Bayfield, WI 54814

First Printing: May 2014

Library of Congress Control Number: 2014941243

ISBN: 978-0-9892399-0-5

TABLE OF CONTENTS

The Harbor City Waterfront
Robert J. Nelson Collection

This photo projects an image of Boutin & Mahan, A. Booth & Sons Fish Packing Company dock sites, Frank Boutin's mercantile store, the Island View Hotel with the Presbyterian Church in the background, circa 1897. The tugs starting on the left, *N. Boutin*, *S.B. Barker* and *R.W. Currie* are tied to the dock about to take on passengers.

Introduction

The phrase "New Wisconsin", and often the name "Indianhead County", printed by the publishers and editor corps in the early 1870's aptly distinguishes Bayfield, Ashland, Iron and Douglas Counties from the populated cities and industrially developed eastern, central and southern counties of the state. This book is a composite of transcribed newspaper reviews from the local publishers documenting life in the Apostle Islands, Bayfield Peninsula, Chequamegon Bay and South Shore of Lake Superior. All stories and tales the reader is about to study, were offered by the weekly six column publications are derived from those very pioneer editors, general news "Squibbers", early settler guest writers and columnar contributors. Some articles appeared nearly 156 years ago.

Since no person had published a document similar to the format herein followed in the transcribed form. Earliest on the name, "Harbor City" was established in the *Bayfield Press* newspaper and appeared intermittently in local and regional papers until the late 1920s, and as this writing now has come full circle. Now...Welcome to *Harbor City Chronicles: The People & Culture*, an account of old Bayfield which relays forward the written newspaper communiques of the time period 1857 to 1927. By no means intended to be academic in nature, subject matter transcribed is never the less accurate as it draws references from the earliest printed history. The community at large, commercial fishing, the pinaries, agriculture, tourism, railroading, legend, lore, and tragedies of the pioneer village are brought to life. A chronological history, enlisted from the works of local scholars of the area, and an index are also provided.

So from what source did I retrieve the stories? The privilege was mine to review hundreds of editions of local Bayfield press corps newspapers stacked on storage shelves at the Bayfield Heritage Association, R. D. Pike Archives. From this magnificent depository assembled were ancient publications of the *Bayfield Mercury* of 1857, *Bayfield Press* of 1870's, *Bayfield County Press* of 1882-1920s and the *Bayfield Progress* from 1906 to 1927. Within the confines of dusky tabloid exterior covers laid a treasure trove of local history waiting for the chance to shine their stories again. The pages jumped to life with regional folklore, fables and facts. Perspective and insight into a lifestyle of the "New Wisconsin" peoples, Chequamegon Bay inhabitants, the" movers and shakers", capitalists, entrepreneurs, and immigrants were introduced in frank and plainspoken print by the publishers. Tattered, frayed, and fragile documents, these fifteen by twenty-two inch, dark-browned protective jacket covered newspapers were at the disposal of a history detective looking for a good story. I was thinking that if I loved to read these chronicles and anecdotes, maybe the public would like the content shared. At the very least, these wonderful stories would pass on to a new set of history detectives.

The task of transcribing and editing 414 short stories to date was enormous, but equally imposing was layout and middle-man duties. So, for six years I sat reading these newspapers, transcribing, contemplating and pondering if I should venture my efforts toward print. As I worked I noticed that not much life or further man-handling of the pages could be had in the old newspapers. As such the wonderful history they relay will render their content inaccessible to future generations or maybe to just a handful of historians, maybe to just a handful of historians. My goal and mission then became one to document and store as many of the good stories that I humanly could put to paper and on my hard drive. This history, the good, bad and even ugly, must be shared with public-at-large for generations to come.

The reader should also consider that *Harbor City Chronicles* takes a different approach than a Mark Twain-ist style of story teller would put into words. Few are the adjectives and all stories are transcribed verbatim, printed word for word, comma for comma, semicolon for semicolon, misspell for misspell; as it should be. To correct the pioneer press masters, to change their styles of writing or twist a sentence, to me, would be considered a breach of journalistic admiration. The reader now here-by has access to first hand information, same as would have the local paying subscribers of the times.... "Hot off the press."

Significantly different it is that the chapter layout and stories do not follow a chronological order, but rather dance around, topic by topic, in different time periods. Some of the photos and maps I chose were very old and could not reproduce well, but, never-the-less replicates a view of the pioneering day that gives perspective to the topic. Note that a personal introduction to a story is boldfaced. The newspaper "*Press*" release introductions to articles are offered in *italic* and **bold** face while the stories themselves are laid out in unadorned type. Sources are listed.

Dedication

Harbor City Chronicles: The People and Culture; Apostle Islands–Bayfield Peninsula–Chequamegon Bay; a Journalistic with Photos is dedicated to long-time "old-families" friend Scotten Knight Hale. Facilitating publication of his cousin Eleanor Knight's *Tales of Bayfield Pioneers: a History of Bayfield*, with Scott and the *Tales* team was a wonderful experience and great pleasure. Scott's suggestion to convey additional stories of Bayfield's vivid and vibrant past to print is what inspired me to make available these stories of the rich history of the people and culture in the "New Wisconsin".

Acknowledgments

My sincerest thanks to the Bayfield Heritage Association's Pike Research Center, and its Board of Directors located at 30 N. Broad Street, Bayfield, Wisconsin for allowing the author access to the archives whose vast collection of local newspapers, historical documents, photos and maps allowed me to share the rich history of the Harbor City with the people of this great state and nation.

The author appreciates the work of the Apostle Islands Historic Preservation Conservancy, a not-for-profit entity established in 2006 to be a hands-on organization that seeks to preserve, maintain and protect historic landscapes within the Apostle Islands National Lakeshore and Northwest Wisconsin.

Chapter One
Pioneer Perspectives

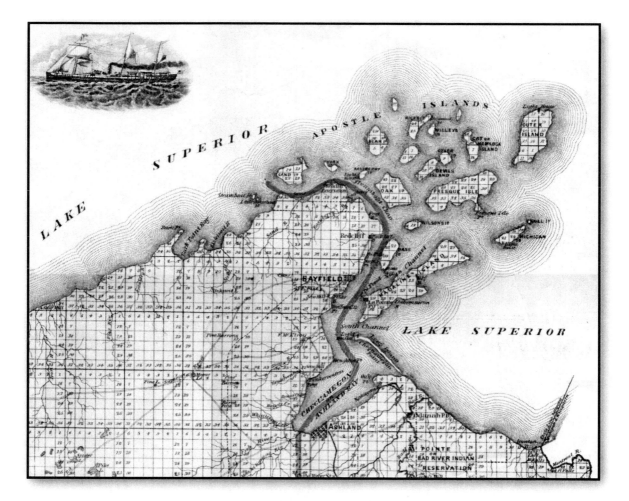

Northern Bayfield & Ashland Counties
1877 Snyder, Van Vechten & Company
Robert J. Nelson Collection

Judge Joseph McCloud
BHA Pike Research Center Archive Collection

Judge Joseph McCloud

The subsequent speech delivered by Judge Joseph McCloud reflects directly to the early settlement of the Western Lake Superior region including Bayfield, Chequamegon Bay, and La Pointe in the "New Wisconsin" along with a few mentioned points of interest located in Minnesota. This speech was conveyed to the people of Bayfield, at a "Lyceum", held "some 12 years ago", circa 1859, by the Judge, who was at that time a resident of this place. Re-printed in 1871 this piece of pioneer journalism laid out a general history of the western end of Lake Superior.

In the *Bayfield County Press* Saturday, December 1, 1900 is offered the obituary of Judge McCloud which states, "he died at the home of Mr. B. A. Brown, on a Wednesday night, after an illness of three weeks. Judge McCloud has made Bass Island his home for a number of years. In his younger days he was very prominent at Washington, District of Columbia, and in this section of the country for many years. He was one of the earliest settlers in Northern Wisconsin. During his early days here he was in Judge and in the hardware business."

The *Washburn Times* in writing of Judge McCloud in the November 14th, 1899 issue states: "Perhaps very few people know who Judge McCloud is, whose life is slowly ebbing away. Thirty-five years ago he was one of the most prominent men in Northern Wisconsin, and was one of the first District Attorneys of LaPointe County. LaPointe County was then pretty much of everything in Northern Wisconsin. Later he held other county offices and was for a long time county judge. Now he is a very old man, and has for many years lived alone on Bass Island, near Bayfield, holding the titles, it is said, for certain property holders, who have furnished him with provisions about once a week. Here the old man lives a hermit life, shut off from the outside world, and all alone on the little island. Very few boats stop over at Bass Island. But occasionally a private yacht or sail boat goes to the place. Two or three times the writer has visited the place and met the venerable old Judge. He is a feeble old man, and has long been in his second childhood. His sight is almost gone, yet he has managed to do his own cooking and take care of his own house. The old man has an organ and a cat - his only companions. Upon the approach of visitors the cat takes to the woods, and to all appearances is almost wild, except to the caresses of the feeble old man. The Judge imagines he is quite a composer, and delights to play original selections on the dilapidated old organ for his friends or visitors. The poor old man is in his dotage and when death comes to him it will no doubt be a welcome visitor. He is one of last of the old men, who in the early days was prominent in the affairs of Northern Wisconsin."

Twould be risky business for the author to assign Judge McCloud notoriety of being Bayfield's first historian, but that as an intellectual of scholarly disposition and adjudicator of civil governance he certainly stands his ground. Hereafter the reader meets the arbitrator of Chequamegon Bay justice in the prime time of his life.

Bayfield Pioneers N. Willey, Geo. Stahl, N. LaBonte, J. Andreas, J. D. Cruttenden, A. Tate, Jos. McCloud
BHA Pike Research Center Archive Collection

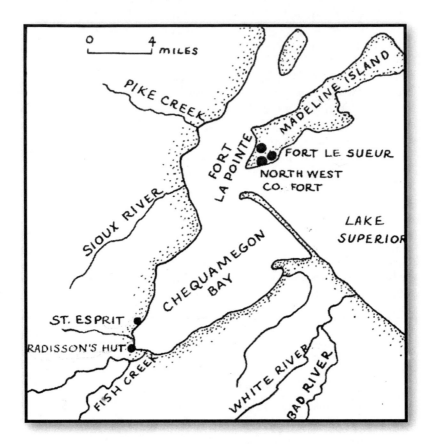

Chequamegon Bay in the New Wisconsin Circa 1659
BHA Pike Research Center Archive Collection

The following three articles are historical accounts of days long gone articulated by citizens who walked the streets of Bayfield up to near to 150 years ago. The topical content relays a superlative overview of the New Wisconsin and Bayfield Peninsula region and its constituency. Judge Joseph McCloud, Publishers R. W. Hamilton and Alonzo Hatch, Louis Wachsmuth and Irwin R. Nye and Bayfield's darling daughter of the 1880s Lillian Tate-Wilkenson create the visual portal into which a reader may slip the time machine to periods ne'er to be taken part in, only brought to consideration.

Early History of the Lake Superior Region

By Judge Joseph McCloud

Bayfield Press - **March 11, 1871**

In reading the history of the world we cannot avoid noticing that certain periods are pretty eminently distinguished by the great actions of men, periods when the whole civilized world appeared moved by an impulse perhaps of conquest, perhaps of discovery and perhaps of religion. Eras of enterprise or man's blood seem to know no feeling but activity, their soul's desire but the accomplishment of memorable dates. We have seen these days of action which were most generally bloody and tumultuous, succeeded by years of calm, peaceful and of striking events that we could almost believe the fire in man's blood has gone entirely out.

The Age of Louis XIV of France was one of striking interest in the worlds history; a spirit of adventure possessed all the civilized governments of Europe; discovery after discovery was made of new regions, and the glowing and romantic accounts published of their riches, beauty and strange inhabitants, was the all absorbing topic from the princes to the peasant. It has not been strange that the monarchs of Europe should desire to possess the lands whose wealth was represented to be incalculable, and from such sources re-establish their depleted treasuries; still less remarkable is that of the society of the Jesuits, whose missions at that time covered the known world, and who began to hope for a blessing that was to be expected on the full firm and of the command of the Savior to preach the gospel.

I remark it is still strange, that this society should take the liveliest interest in these discoveries, either most active in making them, and the first to project new ones. And although it is difficult to tell who displayed most zeal, the trader or the missionary, it is not a hard matter to say whose motives command our admiration, whose memory our respect, who sufferings in devotions our sympathy is held in esteem. So we find the members of this society hand-in-hand with the government in these discoveries; accompanying every expedition, as objective in accomplishing many of their own, establishing missions at every point; doing all in their power for the benefit of the savages, and opposing from that day to this with all their might, the introduction of ardent spirits among them. It is impossible to look at the labors of these men, without admiration, who bore the cross to the banks of the St. Mary, and the confines of Lake Superior and looked wistfully towards the home of the Sioux Indian in the Valley of the Mississippi, five years before Apostle Eliot had addressed the peoples that dwelt within six miles of Boston Harbor.

And Dr. Neal says, "Some years before the Puritan Robinson landed on the icy coast of Plymouth, the disciples of St. Francis had penetrated the forest, even to the waters that empty into Lake Huron. Before the *Mayflower*, with their precious freight, weighed anchor from Southampton, there was a French settlement at Québec. Before Harvard University was in operation, the disciples of Ignatius Loyola were establishing educational institutions on the banks of the St. Lawrence River, and the renowned Richelieu assisted to endow a public hospital under the care of the Ursulines."

As early as 1634 two priests, Brefoef and Daniel erected a mission on the shores of Lake Huron; and in 1641 priests of the same order passed through the river Ottawa, coasted along the shores of Lake Huron to visit by invitation the old Jew boys at the outlet of Lake Superior.

A voyage of 17 days, they arrived at the Falls of St. Marie where they found assembled two thousand of that tribe. Here they learned much and calculated to influence the seal of their society, but it was not until 1654, 13 years after the two adventurous young men, engaged in deferred trade followed the Indians on their hunting excursions for two years and are probably the first white men who gazed on Lake Superior.

They returned to Québec, giving such glowing accounts of this great inland sea that even the Bishop of Québec volunteered to be the first to plant the symbol of his faith among the newly discovered tribes. It was at length determined that the aged Menard, with much experience among the Indians of Western New York, should be the first missionary to go to the shores of Lake Superior. I cannot do better than give the words of Dr. Neal in speaking of Menard, he says: "his hair whitened with age, his mind ripened by long periods, and acquainted with the peculiarities of Indian character, he had been the man for the mission." The night before he started the eyes of the venerable priest were not closed. He thought much of his friends, and knowing that he was about to go into a land of barbarians, two hours after midnight he penned the following letter to a brother missionary.

"Reverend Father— The peace of Christ be with you. I write to you probably the last word, which, I hope will be the seal of our friendship until eternity. Love whom the Lord Jesus did not disdain to love; to the greatest of sinners; for he loves whom he loathes with the cross. Let your friendship, good father, be useful to me by the desirable fruits of your daily sacrifice.

In three or four months you may remember me at the moment for the dead on account of my old age, my weak constitution and the hardships that weigh amongst these tribes. Nevertheless I am in peace, for I have not been led to this mission by any temporal mode, but I think it was by the voice of God. Eternal remorse would have tormented me, had I not come when I had the opportunity. We have been little surprised, not being able to provide ourselves with vestments, and other things; but we will face such as little birds enclose the lilies of the fields, will take care of the servants, and then that it should happen that we should die with one, we would esteem ourselves happy.

I am loaded with affairs. All I can do is to recommend our journey to your daily sacrifices, and to embrace you with the sentiments of heart as I hope to do in eternity. My Reverend Father- your most humble and affectionate servant in Jesus Christ." R. Menard

From the Three Rivers, this 27th of August, two o'clock after midnight 1660, Dr. Neal continues, "this letter is touching in its simplicity and could hardly have been written by one who had not been filled with the spirit of Jesus, and as soon as a Christian people begin to dwell upon the shores of Lake Superior it will be involved in their literature, and read and admired by those whose tastes are refined."

Menard's anticipations were realized; in a few months he was added to "the memento of death." Immediately after he penned this letter he started with a band of Ottawa for Lake Superior, and underwent great hardships on the journey reaching on 15 October the bay which he named St. Theresa, and is supposed to have been the Bay of Keweenaw. After a residence of faith for eight months, amid piles of ice and snow, and with his life in hand he accepted the invitation of some Huron, according to Charlieoux, to go to their island home at LaPointe, then called by them Chewamigan and, by Menard, the Isle of Saint Michael. He commenced his journey accompanied by a faithful man named John Greerer with the service of the missionary many years. On 20, August 1661, being obliged to walk some distance in order to avoid rapids, and while his old servant was making the portage with this canoe, he entered the woods and was lost. To this day it is unknown whether the aged man perished from starvation, or by violence from the savages. But there appears to be well grounded hope that the provenance which feeds a little bird in the desert and encloses the wild flowers of the forest he became a shepherd and that when he came to die he was enabled to dwell with profit on the following sentences of his well found breviary: "the Lord is my shepherd."

On the news of the death of this little man reaching Quebec, Claude Allouez, also a Jesuit, volunteered to continue the labors ended in a so melancholy manner, and reached the shores of Lake Superior in 1665; pushing beyond Ontonogon, he did not stop until he reached the island of LaPointe, the ancient residence of the of the Chippewa. During his residence here he was the first white man to hear of the existence of the great river which he calls Mississippi. His laborers were so successful, that he returned to Québec for assistance, and caring there on but two days he was on return accompanied by a fellow laborer named Nicholas. In 1668 they were joined by Dablon and Marquette; the latter afterword renowned for his discovery of the Mississippi River. Speaking of the mission says Bancroft, "on the shores of the bay to which the abundant fisheries attracted crowds, the channel so rose and the mission of the Holy Spirit was founded. The admiring throngs, who had never seen a European, came to gaze on the white man, and on the pictures which he displayed of the realms of hell in of the last judgment. There a choir of chapel was taught to chant the patter and the eye."

Allouez became weary of the obstinate unbelief of the savages and left the mission in 1669, Marquette taking his place, who speaks of the attack of the Sioux and the Huron's and all of LaPointe in 1670; and in 1671 the mission was abandoned on account of the war raging between these tribes; and the lake was left without a white resident; the Sault Ste. Marie was the nearest French settlement. Here the mission house was burned in 1674 in a conflict between the Sioux.

Although the missionaries appear to have abandoned Lake Superior at this time, it is not so for the trader; for we find Sueur Daniel Duluth an intelligent and enterprising man from Lyon's, in the year 1678 establish a first trading post on Lake Superior, at the mouth of Pigeon River; and towards the end of July 1680 accompanied by five men he crossed from the lake to the Mississippi meeting Hennepin at his camp on the St. Francis, now Elk River. Duluth undoubtedly deserves the credit of being the first white man making this tour. He also appears to have discovered Mille Lacs and caused the Kings arms to go where no Frenchman had ever been and at two other villages of the Sioux 120 leagues further – almost reaching the Red River of the North. Duluth is considered the discoverer of Minnesota; he was a brave soldier, and took an active part in the war between the English and the French in 1687, being a commander at Fort Frontenac, where he died in 1710.

We have an account of Le Sueur being commissioned by Frontenac to establish a post at La Pointe in 1693. But I can find no account of his ever going there and it is hardly probable he went as we find in the month of September 1718, Captain St. Perrie, with Ensign Linctot, who had succeeded St. Pierre, was ordered by presence, in the promise of the missionary, to endeavor to detach the Dakotas from their alliance with the Fox tribes.

At this time Linctot made arrangements for peace between the Ojibway and the Sioux and sent to them Frenchman to dwell in the villages of the latter, with the promise that if they ceased to fight the Ojibway they should have regular trade and a priest to reside with them. At this early date a French officer was commissioned to open a northern route to the Pacific and going westward from the Grand Portage at Lake Superior to Lake Winnipeg. Ascending the Assiniboine, he struck out on the plains and for several days journeyed towards the Rocky Mountains. Here he established some six commercial ports on the road, but difficulties with the Indians forced him to return.

About 1745 the English influence which had been constantly increasing began to assume an appearance of actual hostility; and not only were the French voyageurs robbed and maltreated on Lake Superior, but even then the commandant at Mackinac was exposed to insolence, and there was no security anywhere.

It was not long before Canada was fairly enveloped in a war within New York and New England colonies. I cannot in this lecture give a history of this war as neither my time nor your patience would permit, but we will notice that in 1748 La Rhonde started for LaPointe, and Veranderri for Fond du Lac, to prevent by their presence the dissatisfaction of the Indians, in the incursions of the English.

At the end of the war and after the disturbance of commerce incidents, trade with the Indians again became an object and in 1776 traders left Mackinac, and proceeded as far as the Pigeon River. Thomas Curry ventured as far as the Valley of Saskatchewan and James Finley established a post in the same valley as high as the 48.5° of latitude. This excited the curiosity of the Hudson Bay Company, who tried to counteract the enterprise with private traders; in 1780 the Indians destroyed a post on the Assiniboine, and later plotted to extirpate the traders; but the smallpox breaking out among them prevented the massacre. The Northwest Fur Company was founded in 1783 with 16 shares, entrusted to the management of the brothers Frobisher and McTavish at Montréal. There being dissatisfaction among some, an opposition company was formed after a keen rivalry was merged in the Northwest in 1786. From that time the fur trade of the Northwest became systemized, two agents at Montréal received the goods from England, and two went every year to Grand Portage to receive packs shipped for Europe.

In 1798 the company reorganized at the close of the last century and had in their employee, 50 clerks, 75 interpreters and 1120 canoes. In July the voyageurs began to assemble at Grand Portage to settle accounts and receipts at the new office, and at times more than 1000 were assembled together. The proprietors, clerks, guides and interpreters all met in one large hall, at different tables, and the labors of the day being over, the fiddlers were brought in and were looked forward to with pleasure by the trader at the lonely outpost.

In 1784 we find Alexander Henry with his clerk Perrault arriving at La Pointe from Montréal, and soon after reaching Fond du Lac, where at this time Default was clerk of the Northwest Company, appears to of had a partner named Harris whom he met at this place, where they traded during the winter; and in a drunken quarrel was stabbed in the neck by an Indian, and starting for Montréal for medical assistance, died after passing Mackinac.

The Treaty of 1783 between Great Britain and the United States provided that the British traders and settlers should be allowed to enjoy all their former privileges without becoming citizens of the United States; and the Northwest Company taking advantage of this clause, not only established posts all over Minnesota but even created civil chiefs among the Indians to whom they presented the colors and metals of his Britannic Majesty. Not until the year 1805 were these difficulties put at rest by Congress by passing a law that no foreigner should engage in union trade without becoming a citizen.

In 1809 John Jacob Astor organized the American Fur Company, making their principal post on Lake Superior at LaPointe, while the Northwest and Hudson Bay Companies were engaged in one of the most barbaric quarrels which ever disgraced humanity, a quarrel whose deeds of atrocity would shame the very savages they sneered at. The American Fur Company reports their business reaping a rich harvest; and before the belligerent parties had made peace, secured all that was worth having of the trade. We now see a difference in the manner of doing business on the lake. The fleets of canoes no longer start on their voyage, delayed by every wind, encumbered with their hundreds of voyageurs, coasting along the points and bays, and being months making a trip.

Sailing vessels, one after another, made their appearance. The Northwest Company at the beginning present century had four sailing vessels on the lake. The schooner *Bearu* which was lost at Whitefish Point in 1811; the *Otter*, lost on Terrible Island; the *Mink* lost at the Sioux Rapids, and the brig Recovery which was run over the rapids in 1813, were property of this company. The American Fur Company built the brig *Astor* in 1835 at the Sault Ste. Marie. The schooner *Whitefish* was built at the Sault in 1837, and owned by the Hudson Bay Company. The American Fur Company built the schooner *Brewster* at Sault Ste. Marie in 1838, and the *Siskowit* at LaPointe in 1839; the last named was lost in the Chocolate River in 1853. The brig *Napoleon*, an afterward propeller, was built at the Sault Ste. Marie in 1849. And Captain Bayfield, of her Majesty's Royal Navy, surveyed in the schooner *Bullfrog* from 1821 to 1825.

To the middle of the present century there appears to have been but one object of trade of Lake Superior. Fur, with a grand production of the country; and this so entirely was controlled by companies who could, and did monopolize them, that there was no encouragement for private traders to come here; the mineral wealth of the mountains would attract the eyes of the world, while then undisturbed; and not known of them but by hearsay of the most fabulous nature; it is not strange that in the year 1836 there should be about 130 white inhabitants living on Lake Superior. The settlements on the lake at that time were, commencing at the Sault Ste. Marie; first one trader at Sand Island, one trader at L' Anse, and a Methodist missionary; one trader at Iron River; the American Fur Company supposed at LaPointe, and the missionary, Mr. Hall; the American Fur Company supposed at Fond du Lac, and Bishop Baraga as missionary; the same company also having supposed at Grand Portage. Fort William, the Hudson Bay Company post; Miscihicoten River, the post of the Northwest Fur Company, and at Badgawaming, 60 miles above the Sault Ste. Marie.

With the exception in Fort William, these places were but mere posts in charge of one man with the stock of such goods as the Indians were in the habit of exchanging for furs. Among the American fur traders, LaPointe was looked to with about the same feeling as an interior countrymen thinks of New York and the Emperor of Haydee Hurley demanded or received greater honors, then the company's agent at LaPointe; it was the Mecca of the voyageurs hopes, the place where he made his yearly pilgrimage, where he could get everything he needed and a good man had the privilege of getting drunk once a year; and after a short but pleasant visit, he would take up his pack with a light heart and start forward from the lonely outpost, as happy as any man in the world, with cornmeal and tallow for his food, and sometimes tea to drink, but not always. These days have passed away; it is a rare treat now to hear the voyageurs song timing to the dip of his paddle to the course of a dozen voices, echoing along the Rocky shores of Get-chi-giom-mi, and it is indeed a great location that gathers together enough Indians for dance.

About the year 1840 the mineral resources of the lake began to be develop, mining companies formed as surveys by competent geologists were made and when the immense richness of these mines was first published it produced excitement in a series of successful and unsuccessful speculation unprecedented. The rapid influx of immigration made a larger number of vessels indispensable and in the year 1837 the schooner *Algonquin* was hauled over the Sioux portage, and launched on Lake Superior. In 1840 the schooner *Elizabeth* followed; in 1843 the *Swallow*; in 1844 the *Chippewa*, the *Uncle Tom* and the propeller *Independence*, the first steam vessel on the Lake. In 1845 the schooner

Florence and the steamer *Julia Palmer* were the first side wheel steamers on the Lake. In 1847 the propeller *Monticello*; in 1850 the steamer *Baltimore;* in 1851 the steamer *Sam Ward*; and in 1852 the steamer *Illinois* passed the canal at Sault Ste. Marie, opening a continuous communication between the largest body of fresh water in the world and the Atlantic.

That the increased development of the country could warrant such an augmentation of vessels was of course very great, new mines were starting, new companies forming and new town springing up every month, the difficulty appeared to be to say what there was not. Missions, both Protestant and Catholic, were started on all sides; the Protestant mission at LaPointe under Mr. Hall, being the first. Mr. Hall and wife arrived at La Pointe, August 30, 1831, traveling from Mackinac in an open boat, in the company with Mr. Warren, at that time in charge of the fur companies post. Mr. Ayer also accompanied them and took charge of the school which was immediately established, but the next year Mr. Ayer removed to Sandy Lake and was succeeded by Mr. Boutwell. The Roman Catholic mission was soon after established and the first chapel built at the bridge. The mission at Bad River was established many years ago by Mr. Wheeler and wife, assisted by Ms. Spooner.

The County now increases so rapidly in population and importance that we find it difficult to trace its successive steps. The first mining operations on the lake commenced in the vicinity of Fort Wilkin, in what was called the black oxide theme in the year 1840, and Copper Harbor was started at the same time. In 1841 the Eagle River diggings, now the Phoenix mine, was commenced, and so ore was found for the first time in any quantity, the excitement was great in Eagle River and became a town the same year. Eagle Harbor was also started at this time on the strength of mines opening in this vicinity. Ontonogon was started in 1843 and has become one of the most populous and important places on the lake. Marquette, now the most flourishing town on the lake was commenced in 1849, although a settlement had been made at Carp River a few years earlier. In less than 10 years she is employing hundreds of sail vessels, has a railroad, and is growing in the very times of pressures and panics. Superior was commenced in 1853 and up to the time of the panic, was a miracle of progress.

In 1840 half a dozen little schooners were amply sufficient to carry on the business of the great trading monopolies, and the two or three hundred white inhabitants of Lake Superior, had now increased to many thousand people, engaged in every branch of industry; mining, farming, trading, manufacturing, preaching, teaching, doctoring and lawering; with churches, schools and courthouses; with lyceum's and libraries; emigrants from nearly all corners of the globe; with resources so far developed that they may well be considered inexhaustible, with the healthiest claim on the globe and no longer the wild savages to make them afraid, for on this onward march of the restless Caucasian race, the red monarch of the wood and waters, almost without a murmur retreats farther and farther towards the setting sun.

We have thus glanced rapidly over some of the leading incidents of the discovery in settlement of Lake Superior, we have given you a short history of the past, imperfect and incomplete certainly but to show how wealth and resources may lie undeveloped for centuries; the object which first attracted attention are in reality the least important. The thousands of savage conversions early Jesuits underwent so much are nearly gone, what remained present are anything but an encouraging field for influence of Christianity; in the fur trade which was considered a source of such great importance that nobility encouraged.

Is it now hardly worth notice the cargoes of copper and iron, and agriculture neglected as it has been is of even more importance than the business which at one time was the envy of the commercial world. Comparing what has been with what is, may not pardon predicting the future such as our hearts desire, or even greater than any of us have anticipated very such things that have happened in the last 20 years blaming not the next 20, witnessing equal progress? Why not the iron horse shrieking your populous cities, hundreds of docks being crowded by thousands of vessels, our markets overflowing with produce from the surrounding country, our inhabitants numbered by tens and tens of thousands, our schoolhouses become colleges, our churches, cathedrals, our dwellings, palaces, our cities renowned not only for the rapid growth and commercial prosperity; but the integrity of their people, their institutions of learning and benevolence. Enterprise in order; these things all may be.

We are strong in the faith and we believe they will be, and in future years when none of the oldest have since gathered to talk over the times, when the Lake Superior region contained a few hundred people, they will look back to these as the good old times, and congratulate each other and as their lot should have been cast in this healthful and prosperous section, where they enjoyed so much comfort and so many blessings; for happiness is not so often found in the possession of wealth, luxuries, power as with those would've felt some privations, suffered some hardships, and overcome by many difficulties."

Their day is o'er
Their fires are out from shore to shore,
No more for them the wild deer bounds
Their plough is on their hunting grounds,
The pale man's axe rings through their woods,
The pale man's sails skim o' er their floods
Their pleasant springs are dry;
The children look by power oppressed,
Beyond the mountains of the West,
Their children go to die.

Harbor City, Wisconsin Circa 1897
Burt Hill Collection
RJN-BH-001.20

By the shore of Hiawatha's and Henry Wadsworth Longfellow's *Big Sea Shining Waters*, Lake Superior, on March 24, 1856, in the then village of Bayfield, in the Township of La Pointe a surveyor's boundary stake was driven. This location could likely be where the stake was pounded at the foot of Washington Avenue near to where the *Mackinaw*, on the left, is pulled ashore.

The first newspaper published in the original Townsite of Bayfield, newly christened as the Harbor City by Bayfield founder, Minnesota Territorial Senator- Henry Mower Rice, was the *Bayfield Mercury*.

A weekly, the *Mercury*, on April 18, 1857, printed its first edition and thereafter was published for about a year. To Bayfield by steamer from Sault St. Marie and by wagon teams or stagecoach from Pigs Eye Island in St. Paul on the *Bayfield*-St. Croix Trail would come land speculators, company men, shop and barkeepers, woodsmen, fishermen, lawyers, teachers and entrepreneurs as result of this marketing ploy.

The following is the first of numerous sales pitches from R. W. Hamilton and Alonzo Hatch, along with five additional snippets.

Paddle Steamer *Lady Elgin*
Photo: WikiCommons

The Harbor City Reviewed

By R. W. Hamilton & Alonzo Hatch

Bayfield Mercury - April 18, 1857

Bayfield is situated on the shore of Lake Superior, opposite or near the Apostle Islands, in La Pointe County, Wisconsin, eighty miles below Superior City. It is not quite two years since this town was laid out, and yet so rapidly has it grown that it now actually contains a population of nearly six hundred persons with many good substantially constructed buildings, among the most important and useful of these was a large steam saw mill, erected about a year ago by Mr. John Caho, of Washington, but was unfortunately burnt down in January last. Mr. C., however, not the least daunted by this misfortune, left town a few days after for the purchase of other machinery which will be set up in active operation in a few weeks.

There is a regular line of large and commodious steamers running from Detroit to this place, one from Buffalo and another from Chicago. There will also be established during the coming summer a daily line of coaches between this point and St. Paul, and by the 10th of July, 1859, it will be connected with Madison, Wisconsin by means of a railroad now under course of construction.

Bayfield is not by any means a matter of speculation, but a matter of fact, of utility, the wants of the country demand it, and nature has performed its every duty towards it in providing every requisite necessary to supply those wants. We think it is not too much to say that Bayfield, among other advantages, has the largest, safest and best harbor on the lake. The water is deep, it is easy of access, and perfectly safe when inside.

Bayfield is the county seat of La Pointe County. It is rich in mines, abounding with timber, and possesses an agricultural country back of it that cannot be surpassed even in the renowned British provinces of Canada, or the far famed Valley of the Genesee.

It may be argued by some that Bayfield is a long way north and it must of necessity, therefore, be cold. This is a mistaken notion, its immediate proximity to those large bodies of water in combination with other local circumstances render it a very agreeable, congenial and healthful climate.

The country here is rich in natural advantages, and the climate is such as to confer on its inhabitants the choicest and most valuable blessing that any people can enjoy, viz: good health. What is so much to be prized as a sound and vigorous body and mind?

The Superior country has decidedly one of the healthiest climates of any territory in the Northwest — again, it is a delightful place to live, to enjoy life. This vast expanse of water, where nature has performed her proudest works to make things lovely, with all the real comforts and luxuries of life that this new and rapidly growing country affords in connection with the beautiful scenery of those Islands, and the lovely shore and banks of Lake Superior. Who will not enjoy life here? Who will not be content and happy? All, all! All that have ever visited those shores heretofore, have loved them, have delighted to wander along their banks and cull sweet flowers from their brow, and all, who in years to come, that may chance to find their way here will exclaim with high enthusiasm: — this is one of nature's loveliest spots.

In the June 30 edition the *Mercury* reports that a "meeting was held at the office of the newspaper "pursuant to previous notice for the purpose of nominating a suitable person for Judge of La Pointe County", to be supported at the ensuing election. The meeting was called to order by appointing Mr. John Hanley, Esquire, as Chairman. On motion, Joseph McCloud, Esquire was unanimously nominated as candidate for County Judge. On motion, the Chair appointed the following persons as a canvassing committee: John Hanley, Benjamin F. Bicksler, James Chapman, and Samuel S. Vaughan. Resolved, that the proceedings of this meeting be published in the *Bayfield Mercury*. The meeting adjourned, *sine die-* John Hanley, President, A. J. Steadman, Secretary; June 30, 1857.

In the July 4, 1857 edition, the *Mercury* states, "Bayfield is situated on the shore of Lake Superior, opposite or near the Apostle Islands, in La Pointe county, Wisconsin, eighty miles below the Town of Superior. It takes its name from Lieutenant Bayfield, the English navigator, who made the first survey of Lake Superior some fifty years ago, and whose chart still remains the only correct and reliable one before the public.

The town was surveyed and platted by William McAboy, Esquire, for the proprietors in the spring of 1856, one year ago. Immediately after the completion of the survey, the company, then consisting of Honorable Henry M. Rice, of Minnesota; Hugh H. Sweeny and Benjamin F. Rittenhouse, Esquire, of Washington and Charles E. Rittenhouse, Esquire, of Georgetown, D. C., employed Major McAboy as their agent to make certain permanent improvements.

Near this point has been erected a large steam saw mill at an expense of $10,000. Just above the mill, on the rise of ground in a handsome grove, is now nearly completed a large and magnificent hotel, with sixty-six feet front, with two wings running back from the main body of the building 60 feet, two stories high. The furniture for this hotel was ordered from Cleveland early last spring by Charles E. Rittenhouse, and was brought up on the Steamer *Illinois* is now ready and will in a few days be put into the house.

The company has expended a considerable sum in grading the streets and other general improvements for the benefit of the town. An immense amount of money has already been spent here and yet the real work has only just barely begun. Every hundred dollars now spent, however, will make more apparent improvement, than every thousand at the outset.

The mill commenced to run on the 10th of September last, nine months ago; at that time there was not one frame building completed in the place. Since then, and mostly through the cold weather of the winter, have been built many good, substantial, well finished houses, besides a host of smaller ones. Among the number denominated first class permanent buildings may be found the dwelling house of Major McAboy, 37 by 43 feet, two stories high with cottage roof, costing $3500, which stands on a sightly eminence away to the east of the town, near the bank on the lake, encircled by a handsome group of tall waving trees. — This is certainly one of the most delightful residences that one could find anywhere on the shores of Superior.

Just below this house at the foot of the bluff is the hardware store of McCloud & Brother. The building is 20 by 40 with a twelve foot ceiling, handsomely finished and painted. This store put up at a cost of from $1,000 to $1,200 is now filled with a respectable stock of hardware, cutlery and stoves, with a great variety of other useful articles not strictly belonging to that class of trade. — Next is a store and dwelling of Julius Austrian, 34 by 54, two stories high, finished off in a most handsome style with a neatly built verandah in front. This building, thus completed, costs not less, probably, than $3,500.

Besides those already mentioned is the handsome two story house of Mr. Mathews, Mr. Dunn, Mr. Warren, Mr. Day, Mr. Brown, Mr. Gheen, store and dwelling; Mr. Jordon, Mr. Hanley, Mr. Waggoner, Messrs. Mathews & Sage, house and shop; Mr. Cramer, Mr. Fisher, Mr. Vaughan, Mr. E. S. Dunn, Mr. H. S. Sage, Mr. A. J. Day, Mr. McElroy, Messrs. Hacker & Teemeyer, Mr. Lind, Mr. McLain, Mr. D. H. Austrian, shoe store; Mr. Childs house and office, and Mr. James Freer, and the most important, the Bayfield Exchange, kept by our host Mr. John B. Bono. Mr. B., by the way, is just the man for a landlord. If there is any good things in town, a respectable portion of them are sure to be on his table. The buildings here enumerated are all two stories, are well built, neatly finished and painted. Thus, as though in the morning there was nothing but a wilderness, in the evening a beautiful, bright little town can be viewed.

July 11, 1857: One year ago there was not a frame house in Bayfield, there is now in all, over a hundred, with a population in proportion. We put the figures at as near what they really are as possible, so that when the stranger, the emigrant, lands on our shore, he will not be disappointed, he will not come to us and say that we have misrepresented our true position, and misled them.

August 15, 1857: Charles E. Rittenhouse Esquire, has deeded six lots to the Reverend Alexander Shiras of Chestnut Hill, Philadelphia, in trust for the future permanent Episcopal Church of Bayfield and has given in addition to this $1,000 cash towards the temporary building previous to the completion of the main body of the church. The citizens here have subscribed $600 and are faithfully exerting themselves from day to day for additional subscriptions. Honorable Henry

M. Rice has also deeded a valuable lot besides a liberal cash donation. Any friends of the cause wishing to aid the church in the Northwest can hand in their donations to the Reverend A. Shiras, Philadelphia. Will anything be done in this way? Will our friends at the east show us the smiling face, the friendly hand, the liberal heart? Let us hereafter be able to write the word YES.

The steamer *Lady Elgin*, from Chicago made a trip last week carrying up a large number of passengers. The *Elgin* is a pleasant boat to travel on. Her commander, Captain Thompson, is a real friendly, social man and the Clerk, Mr. Tryan, is one of the pleasantest and most accommodating fellows on the Lake. And then again her second clerk, Mr. Hatch, is a regular brick. He sometimes brings up late papers and sometimes don't.

The school lands will be sold at La Pointe on the 20th inst. A considerable number of disputed claims will come before the commissioners, and we believe from our acquaintance with the Commissioners, that every man having just claims and properly set forth will receive honest, fair attention."

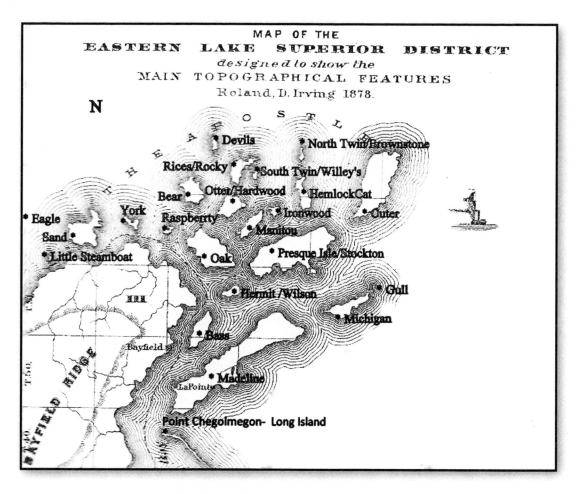

Bayfield Ridge & the Apostle Islands
Robert J. Nelson Collection

Naming of the Apostle Islands

By Louis Wachsmuth-Publisher

Irwin R. Nye-Editor and Manager

Bayfield Progress - November 30, 1917

The naming and re-naming of the Apostle Islands is not so clearly put to paper. From the columns of the *Bayfield Progress*, here follows a generally accepted explanation of how the world famous Apostle Islands names came to be. Responding to a query sent in by H. C. Hale, the *Wisconsin Magazine of History* gave the following interesting story of Apostle Island history and the why of how the names of several islands came to be.

The collective name of Apostle Islands for the group off the coast of Chequamegon Bay is nearly two centuries old. The first map on which they appear is that of Bellin in 1744. This was founded on the information given by Father Pierre Francois Xavier de Charlevoix, a noted Jesuit missionary, who in 1721 visited the western country as an agent for the French Government.

Charlevoix himself did not go into Lake Superior in person, but at Sault St. Marie and Mackinac he made extensive inquiry of competent observers, and noted down the information given him by traders and officers from that region. Thus he, no doubt, learned that the islands were known to the French who frequented that place as the "The Twelve Apostles", and as such they appear on the map of Bellin that was issued in Charlevoix's book published in Paris in 1744.

The first English traveler to note these islands was Jonathan Carver, who coasted the shore of Lake Superior in 1767 and on the map published in his *Volume of Travels* (London, 1778) repeats the name, "Twelve Apostle Islands."

The first American travelers in that region were those who were accompanied by Lewis Cass, who in 1820 made an official voyage along the southern shore of Lake Superior. One of the members was James D. Doty, who was afterwards territorial governor of Wisconsin. In *Doty's Journal*, published in Wisconsin Historical Collections, XIII, p. 201, he says: "The islands called by Charlevoix, the Twelve Apostles, extend about 20 miles from Point Chegoiamegon." Another member of the party was Henry Rowe Schoolcraft, who later became Indian agent at Sault St. Marie, and married a part Indian girl descended from Ojibwa chiefs. Schoolcraft proposed to change the name of the Twelve Apostles to Federation Islands. He assigned to the several islands the names of the states of the Union, giving that of Virginia to Madeline, the largest of the group. Schoolcraft's proposal was not followed, but the present names of York and Michigan Islands remain as part of that proposal.

Apparently the early traders, counting the islands loosely, thought there were twelve in all, and since the mission was "Mission du Saint Esprit the name Twelve Apostles seemed appropriate.

With regard to the several names of separate islands, Outer Island explains itself, as do Ironwood, Oak, Bass, Sand, Rocky, South Twin, North Twin, Bear, Cat, Otter and Raspberry Island takes its name from the Raspberry River. This name was used in its French form Riviere a la Framboise as early as 1804. Devils Island and Manitou Island are both the same name. That is, the Ojibwa called all supernatural beings "Manitou's." Hermit and Stockton Island have probably some local significance from dwellers upon their area.

Madeline Island has been known by many names. Its present name is that of the wife of early trader, Michel Cadotte. She was an Ojibwa woman whose father was a local Ojibwa chief. Madelaine was the name she received when baptized. The island was frequently known as St. Michel or St. Michel's, from the given name of Michael Cadotte, who was the principal trader on the island for many years. The Ojibwa name was Moningwanekaning, to mean the place of the Golden-breasted Woodpecker. However, Father Chrysostom Verwyst, a Catholic missionary, now our best authority on Ojibwa place names, defines it recently in *Acta ET Dicta,* July 1916, published by the Catholic Historical Society of St. Paul, as "the place where there are many lapwings."

The island has also been called La Rhonde, for a French commandant of the eighteenth century; La Pointe Island, from the name of the region called LaPointe du Chequamegon; and

Saint Esprit Island. It was also called Middle Island as lying midway between Sault St. Marie and Fort William, the fur-trade post on the northwest of Lake Superior. Sometimes it appears on the map as Montreal Island; the reason for this we do not know; perhaps it was the terminus of the trip from Montreal, Canada, or was so named because of its inhabitants had been educated at Montreal."

Chapter Two
Meet the Press

Bayfield County Press Printing Office Circa 1897
Burt Hill Collection
RJN-BH-43

Currie G. Bell, Editor-Publisher of the *Bayfield County Press*
BHA Pike Research Center Archive Collection

Bayfield First, the World Afterward

A wonderful promotional and educational role the pressmen and women of the early days of Bayfield played. The champions of the development of village, town and later city, these witty promoters of Bayfield's future wrote with wit and wisdom. Included in their columns were the politics of the day, the who's who of Bayfield, *Local Marine Matters*, departures and arrivals of the transport ships, world events, how to fix it-how to build it columns, church news and a sports column, obituaries, romantic and western novels, and the classics such as Harriet Beecher Stowe's *Uncle Tom's Cabin*.

Many a laborer who came to Bayfield to find prosperity had at best a primary or intermediate educational background; very few graduated from high school. Newspapers were the windows to the world and provided the peoples of the Harbor City and kept all who anteed up the $2 subscription fee in the informational loop. This educational tool derived from with the columns served primary learning and literary needs of near to 2600 residents in 1926, Bayfield's peak population year. Starting with Currie G. Bell at the *Bayfield County Press*, the summaries and salutatory's backtrack. All present insights into newspapers are from 1857 to 1927. The salutatory of the *Bayfield Progress*, published 1906-1927, the author did not locate.

The *Washburn Times* remarks of Currie Bell, the Bay counties senior publisher, "Currie G., print man from Bayfield, who is known as the "tall sycamore from Bayfield" represents his town well. Just why he should be known as the "tall sycamore, is a point we never could make quite clear. He has lived nearly all his life in Wisconsin, and it is a question whether he ever saw a Sycamore. The "tall pine tree", standing about 6'2", would be more appropriate. Currie has represented his town for years – the reason for it being that he always looks out for Bayfield first, the world afterward."

Rival in-town newspaper, the Bayfield Progress, in Bell's obituary states on November 15, 1921 that:

"Currie George Bell was born in Houghton, Maine, July 1, 1852 and died in his home in this city, Sunday afternoon, November 13, 1921 at 4:15 o'clock. He spent the first four years in his native community with his parents who then moved to St. Johns, New Brunswick. At the age of 12 he migrated with his parents from St. Johns to Wisconsin, settling at Marshall. There he attended schools and also the Marshall Academy. When aged 18 he went to the Pennsylvania oil fields, where he remained a little more than a year. Returning to Wisconsin he interested himself in logging activities participating in the great spring log drives on the Fox River for six years.

"He was married at Marshall, Wisconsin to Ada Elizabeth Fuller, on May 7, 1878. Five children blessed this marriage, three still living. Mrs. Bell passed away September 30, 1887. Following his marriage he engaged in newspaper work and established the *Marshall Effort*. In 1879 he purchased the *Waterloo Wisconsin Journal* and published that paper until July, when he sold it, following a brief visit to Bayfield that year. In September 1882 Mr. Bell and his family moved to Bayfield to make their permanent residence and he purchased the *Bayfield County Press*. He remained at the active head of the *Press* until May 1, 1908, when he relinquished active business life, and turned over the publication of the paper to his son, Donald C. Bell.

"Shortly after his removal to Bayfield from Waterloo, he was appointed by President Garfield to the office of receiver for the Bayfield Land Office, which position he held continuously for many years. In 1888 he was one of the presidential electors for the State of Wisconsin and cast the vote of the state in the Electoral College for President Harrison. Under the Harrison administration he was appointed postmaster at Bayfield, which position he held for many years. On December 25, 1890 he was married to Miss Mary A. Roberts, who died August 9, 1906.

"Mr. Bell was a member of the State Fisheries Commission for several years, and to him is due the credit for securing the establishment of the State Fish Hatchery, at Salmo, near this city. He was a member of the Wisconsin Republican Central Committee, was Chairman of the Town of Bayfield for fourteen successive terms and served nine successive years as Chairman of the Board-Bayfield County. He established, located and laid out Greenwood Cemetery, his last resting place. In 1893 he erected the first brick business block in Bayfield [2 N. 2nd Street]. He was a member of the Royal Arch of Masons- Ashland, and the Knights Templar Lodge of Ashland, and the A.F. & M of Bayfield. He is survived by three children, Mrs. H. Lamont, Mrs. E.L. Southmayd and Donald C. Bell."

A further introduction to Currie George Bell and his *Bayfield County Press* whose weekly printed newspapers today as "state-of-the-art" in content, quality and quantity seemed a logical place to start. The *Bayfield Mercury*, *Bayfield Republican* and *Bayfield Press* follow.

Currie Bell's Complete Cylinder Printing Press
RJN-BH-032

The Bayfield Townsite Newspaper Corps

By Editor- Currie G. Bell

Bayfield County Press - October 12, 1897

[So writes Editor Bell,] "With this issue of the *Press* the 15th year of publication is completed. A review of these fifteen years will surely show a vast change not only in northern Wisconsin, but also Bayfield County and the town of Bayfield itself. Fifteen years ago not a railroad had penetrated thus far and the few small towns on Lake Superior were considering whether it was best to hang on a while longer or move to more congenial quarters. But the untiring energy of their inhabitants held them here with a fortunate result.

Then Bayfield had a mail…well whenever it came. Today we have three mails each day and can communicate with our sister towns by telephone. Then street lighting was something that was, while earnestly desired, was seldom had; now our electric lights guide the worry watcher at all hours of the night. Then the Bayfield Hydraulic Company was an infant; now we have two large reservoirs and a force of water sufficient to serve all the portions of the village. Then beyond Broad

Street, Bayfield was practically uninhabited; now lots at the far extremities of the town plat are commanding good prices for residence purposes.

The present editor of this paper came to Bayfield in 1882. At that time facilities for communication with the outer world were but little better than fifteen years ago, while business were confined to a few firms. To enumerate the many changes which have occurred even in the past seven years would take more space than we can give. Suffice to say that a large number of our heavy business firms have located at Bayfield since the *Press* has been under its present proprietorship. Among them we may notice the Bayfield Brownstone Company with a backing of $1 million, and the A. Booth Packing Company with its houses scattered from the Atlantic to the Pacific, while the logging interest are represented by the Corning Lumber Company and Brigham and Mussel, Boutin and Best, Wright and Ketchum, Frank V. Holston, Pike and Drake and numerous others whose operations have practically begun since 1882.

Even at this date Bayfield County consisted of all but one town and Bayfield was the polling place for the entire County. Now we have four town organizations; Bayfield, Washburn, Drummond and Mason, and within these town organizations are numerous thriving settlements. The large lumber firms which do business at these points would each form a suitable article for the *Press* and in time past have received their share of attention in its columns. To say that the aggregate amount of business done in the county has been multiplied by 100 during these years would be putting it very mildly.

A brief review of the *Press* and its history will not, we feel sure, the other place at this period of its existence. From *Industries of Bayfield* we gather the following. "The first paper published in Bayfield was the *Mercury*, in August 18, 1857 by Hamilton and Hatch, who received a bonus from the Bayfield Land Company, composed of honorable Henry M. Rice of St. Paul, H. B. Sweeney, Benjamin F. and Charles E. Rittenhouse and Hamilton G. Fant, Washington DC. This paper was published about one year.

The next newspaper enterprise was the *Bayfield Press*, which made its appearance on October 1, 1859, by Joseph H Campbell of Ontonogon, Michigan with the Rev. William B. McKee, editor, assisted by Joseph McCloud and Cyrus K. Drew, which was published about two years and a half when it was suspended, and the material purchased by Samuel S. Vaughn.

In the summer of 1870 Samuel S. and Hank O. Fifield revived the *Press*, and continued its publication about two years, when it was removed to Ashland June 1, 1877. Sam S. Fifield shortly after moved the office back and commenced the publication of the *Press* with Morris Edwards as the business manager. In the spring of 1879 David L. Stinchfield became editor and conducted business until April 1, 1880, when the office was purchased by Isaac H. Wing, Mr. Stinchfield continuing as editor until the spring of 1881, when he was superseded by D. H. Pulcifer. Mr. Pulcifer shortly after resigned to accept a government position, and then A. C. Stevens wielded the editorial pen until September 30, 1882, when the present proprietor Currie G. Bell purchased the entire plant; enlarged the paper from a six column folio to a five column quarto; also adding a complete job printing outfit."

The present proprietor of the *Press* has nothing but feelings of gratitude toward his many patrons in Bayfield, as well throughout other towns and cities where this paper is read, for their generous support in time past. He only can promise that a constant effort will be made to make the *Press* worth their continued attention, with the assurance on his part that the interest of Bayfield, in the future as the past, will be his first and constant care.

On July 12, 1902 the Bayfield County Press under Publisher Bell reported of a new rival as the headlines read, *The Bayfield Gazette is Launched* and stated, "The *Bayfield Gazette* is the name of a new paper that will be launched upon the journalistic sea next week, with Charles E. Hunt as editor and publisher. Mr. Hunt has secured rooms in the Theodore Ernst building on the corner of Rittenhouse Avenue and First Street, and expects to get out his first number next week, Thursday. Mr. Hunt came to Bayfield with the intention of starting a paper at the new town of Cornucopia, but as things were not in readiness up there for immediate work, he decided on engaging in the newspaper business in this city.

Bayfield Mercury Salutatory

By R. W. Hamilton - Alonzo Hatch

Bayfield Mercury - April 18, 1857

In commencing the publication of a journal like this, as it is customary for editors to salute their readers with a sort of an inaugural address, in which they define, at least to some extent, the moderated position in regard either to politics, morals or religion, or local interests, or anything else, that they intend to occupy in conducting it; and believing that that rule is a good one, we will here proceed to mark out, as it were, the boundary lines by which we intend to run, and briefly allude to some of those measures that will in future claim a portion of our time. In politics, our motto is "THE PEOPLE" and our great aim will be to advocate those measures most nearly allied with their interests, let them come from whatsoever source, party, sect, or creed they may.

We enter, therefore, into the political arena with a perfect freedom of thought and pen; unfettered and untrammeled in every way; possessing the liberty, and certainly imbued with the determination, to strike at error and wrong wherever we may find it; as well as to cherish and do battle for the right with our utmost strength, regardless who may oppose.

It would be a needless waste of time for us to attempt to point out the numberless advantages which must accrue to a young and rising community from the establishment of a paper like ours in their midst. These advantages are doubtless apparent to every intelligent man in our neighborhood; and need not, therefore, be dwelt upon by us. One point, however, we desire our readers to bear especially in mind is that the merits and good qualities of a paper depend, to a very great extent, upon the manner in which they respond to the labors of the publisher. The town of Bayfield is as yet but a small place; indeed, the whole county of La Pointe is, as yet, but thinly settled; we must, therefore, of necessity, throw ourselves more entirely upon the generosity and enterprising spirit of the few, than we otherwise would upon the many. Considering these circumstances, the people of the town will see the importance of individual effort in aid of the present enterprise; and trusting that this effort will be made, we boldly launch our little baroque, and fling to the breeze its virgin flag, — not the less worthy of respect, we trust, from bearing upon its folds the simple inscription, "The People, and the People's Rights," instead of more pretensions and high sounding professions.

BAYFIELD REPUBLICAN

EDITORS—C. MARSH, A. P. BURNHAM.   TERMS $2.00 A YEAR.

Vol. 1.   Bayfield, Dec. 10, 1862.   No. 1.

FELLOW SOLDIERS:—
We have this day begun the publication of a newspaper which is designed for the instruction of each other, believing as we do, that it will both interest and amuse those who are at a loss to know how to pass away the long winter hours without resort to the paste-boards.

from a source which it would not be politic to divulge, that a move is in contemplation, what I am not at liberty to mention, which will have the effect to strike terror to the hearts of the rebels. The enthusiasm for "Little Mac" is unbounded since his masterly advance on Washington. As for me, I know of no event that

BHA Pike Research Center Archive Collection

Bayfield Republican Salutatory

Bayfield County Press - **February 2, 1903**

Fellow Soldiers: –

We have this day begun the publication of a newspaper which is designed for the instruction of each other, believing as we do that it will both interest and use those who are at a loss to know how to pass away the long winter hours without resort to the paste-boards.

It will contain the latest news by telegraph as well as the local news. No pains will be spared to make it a paper for the million. It will be the largest and cheapest newspaper within 50 miles of Bayfield. It will be published every Thursday and will be furnished to each subscriber at two dollars per annum in advance, which, considering the high price of paper is as cheap as we can afford it. We shall strive to advance the interest of the Republican Party, and go in for the vigorous prosecution of the war.

No compromise with traitors. Friends and patrons of the paper will oblige us by handing in such communications as will amuse and instruct, at least two days before the day of publication. No items of indecent character will be inserted and none but original pieces wanted. Ed's

Fellow Soldiers:-

It is with feelings of pleasure mingled with some misgivings that we present to you the first number of the Bayfield Republican. We appreciate your taste and fear that we shall fall short of the standard which upon made your ideal. Yet we are confident that we shall be able to amuse you for a short time, besides giving you an opportunity of writing on different subjects and hearing your communications read, enabling you to understand your capabilities as well as to correct your faults. We are all capable of improvement and culpable if we neglect the means. Let us all work together; that there be a fair and friendly criticisms of everything that appears in the columns of papers, and let all not divulge that a troop move is in contemplation. I am not at liberty to mention, which will have the effect to strike terror into the hearts of the rebels. The enthusiasm for "Little Mac" is unbounded since his masterly advance on Washington.

As for me, I know of no event that has transpired since the Rebellion broke out that has so fully established our beloved general's fame as a strategist, as that masterly retreat. We are having times now, doing nothing. You know what it would be impossible to advance now, as we are not ready, at least so the report says. I suppose that "Mac" hasn't all his plans laid yet, but when he does get them made, and we do move, woe betide the foe!

Three Days Later –

I had just heard of the removal of McClellan and the appointment of Burnside as his successor. Now isn't that glorious news? I have never had a very good opinion of "Mac." He has done nothing since he has had command, but now it will be different. We may look for stirring times soon.

Four days later –

We have spent the past week in taking leave of "Mac." We hope for better times now, for the men are tired of inaction. I can write now. I close with three cheers for Burnside. Yours truly; the Scribble, *Bayfield Republican*, December 6, 1862,

Perusing the *Bayfield County Press*
Dr. Henry Hannum
James and Marge Miller Collection
Courtesy of Marietta LaBonte-Demars

Bayfield Press Salutatory

By Samuel S. & Hank O. Fifield
Owners - Editors - Publishers
Bayfield Press - October 13, 1870

Today, we give to the public, the first number of the *Bayfield Press*, a weekly newspaper devoted to the interest of Lake Superior, and for the purpose of making known the vast resources of this inland sea, bordered by three States and a foreign country, yet its interest are undivided, and as no legitimate aid can be given to one point or interest without benefiting all, we will act accordingly.

We propose to make the *Press* a success, if possible, and our great allure will be to place before the people, the advantages of this rich, but as yet undeveloped region. Our earnest support will be given for the advancement of all plans in this direction, for its early settlement, its railroad interests, its fisheries, and all other local matters connected with this section. The columns of our paper are open to all correspondence, which has anything of importance on the subjects to communicate. We shall, also, endeavor to give good recollections of state and miscellaneous news, and make a first-class family paper – a credit to Bayfield and the State. As an advertising medium, the *Press* will afford superior facilities, at living rates, to all who wish to make known their business through its columns.

Politically, the *Press* will be independent upon all important measures coming before the country – neutral in nothing. As a party organ, however, it may be safely counted out, until our local resources are developed. With these few plainspoken words we make our bow. S. S. Vaughn

Chapter Three
Timber, Fish & Brownstone

Last Log Sawed: Late summer 1927

Wachsmuth Lumber Company- Robert Morrin (L)

BHA Pike Research Center Archive Collection

Captain Robinson Derling Pike
BHA Pike Research Center Archive Collection

Bayfield historian Eleanor Knight had this to say about the Captain: "Captain Pike is the outstanding citizen of Bayfield's first century. His character was well summarized in a county booklet published in 1905 which said, "Captain Pike is a thoroughly progressive man in the fullest sense of the term. He believes that what is good for Bayfield is good for him, and it is not out of place to add that no citizen takes more interest in the building of the community than he does."

Interview with a Veteran Saw Mill Man

Bayfield County Press - March 2, 1889

From the *Bayfield County Press*, July 26, 1890 is stated that, "the Captain is nothing if not romantic and in the early history of this mill he determined that he should always be prepared to make a record that would go ahead of any mill of her capacity on the bay (Chequamegon Bay)."

Hence he named the plant, the "Little Daisy." In this year Captain Pike "let" the operation of the plant to a Mr. McCurdy and Higginson, who superintended sawing activities and to who effected up to 89,980 feet per day, are credited having great success. That the operation was successful both men contended happened for two reasons: the mill within the past three years had been put into good running order by Captain Pike who had spent several thousand dollars, and the second and most important reason for their success is that they employed the best men obtainable for the various positions and paid liberally. On the "scribes" trip through the mill on this day he found that the chief positions were filled as follows: Charles Brooks was the head sawyer; Arthur Jones and Harry Dora, setters, with Ed Gordon as the carriage rider. At the other end of the mill was the old reliable Myron B. Conklin who handled the large resaw. By 1892, the December 17 edition of the *Bayfield County Press* reports Captain Pike "had a force of men at work on Oak Island and will get out several million feet this winter." From amongst the Apostle Islands to inland hillsides of the Bayfield Peninsula, the Pike lumberjacks and teams harvested unimaginable cords of White Pine and hardwoods. The *Press* scribe further reveals the epic story of the "business man of the century."

MORE EARLY HISTORY: R. D. Pike, tells of long shanty days; first mill in this section was located on Pike's Creek – driven by water power – capacity 4000 feet and 24 hours read the headlines on this date.

Captain R. D. Pike, the oldest saw mill man on Chequamegon Bay, and one of the most prominent in business affairs of her city, was interviewed by a *Press* reporter this week and gave out the following facts regarding the early manufacture of lumber in this section:

"We had no band saws, carriages, trimmers, steam niggers [sic], wenches and such like in the old mill that stood on the stream 4 miles from the city in 1855, and when I look back upon that scene I can't help but wonder that the little city of Bayfield ever got its start from the erection of a frame building."

Captain Pike was born in Meadesville, Pennsylvania, in the year 1838 and moved to this section with his parents November, 1855, first landing at LaPointe and then coming to the main shore and settling on the creek that now supplies with the purest of water to the world's greatest fish hatchery. The stream in the bay into which it flows had no name at that time, except that given them by the Indians, which is unpronounceable. Shortly after arrival, however, the stream in the bay which welcomed the sparkling waters took the name "Pike" and has ever held them unto this day.

Here, in the dark shades of a sea of waving pines, not a mile from where is now located the state fish hatchery, resided the veteran lumberman. His home was a shanty of roughly hewn logs, purchased by his father from the American Fur Company, and was located near the place where the "old Pike house" now stands. It was a spot of wild beauty, and one, which we daresay, that Mr. Pike's mind often wanders to as he sits back and rests from the cares and business worries of his life. It was in a wilderness, it is true, but, with the sparkling waters of the silvery stream coursing their way down through a valley of shaded green, and it seemed there came little ripples of laughter that told that nature gloried in her beautiful work.

On the stream stood the old mill, its great paddle-wheel splashing in the foamy waters like a huge fish. It was owned and operated at that time by Austrian & Leopold. In the summer of 1856 Mr. Pike's father purchased the mill and operated it until the close of the Civil War. The machinery was driven by water power and the cuts in 24 hours, if everything went well, would total

4000 feet. When, finally, operations were suspended the old mill went to pieces, parts of it rotting away every year until now there's scarcely a trace of it left.

R. D. Pike enlisted in the Army at Ontonogon in 1862, enrolling in the 27th Michigan Infantry. Later he was promoted to a Lieutenant in the first Michigan Calvary and served as such until nearly the close of the war, was again promoted, this time to Captain commanding a Company at Appomattox. From this latter name place he was sent with his men across the plains to battle against the "Reds" finally being mustered out at Salt Lake City in March, 1866.

In the year 1867 or 68 Pike again entered in to the mill business, this time for himself, at LaPointe. Here he erected a shingle mill and operated the same about a year, when, through the carelessness of one of the employees, it was blown up. The exact cause for the bursting of the boiler will always remain a mystery. The building was blown to atoms, one man killed and another crippled for life. After the destruction of this mill Pike returned to Bayfield and erected a plant. This mill, although it has been remodeled and refitted with modern machinery, is operating today, and is one of the best equipped plants, of its size, for the manufacture of lumber on the bay.

"The town of Bayfield was laid out by William McAboy March 24, 1856,"says Mr. Pike, "and for many years were celebrated at that date, when Andrew Tate and James Chapman were alive, but of late years it has all been dropped."

"During the years of 55 and 56 there were large encampments of the Indians along the shore from Pikes Bay to where the town of Washburn now stands. They were a peaceable lot, however, and nothing was feared from them."

Captain R. D. Pike went to school here for a short time, finishing his education at Toledo and Ypsilanti that fitted him for the great business workings in which he has been connected.

Captain R. D. Pike, who owns and operates the smartest circular mill on the bay, has had a force of men at work ever since the mill closed in December, refitting throughout, and will be prepared to lower his already unprecedented record this coming season. He has put in a new steam boiler, which, with a battery of four boilers, he has heretofore used, will give him an ample supply of steam to run the additional machinery he is putting in; consisting of a Prescott Steam Feed, Steam Nigger [sic] and Murray Slab Slasher. It is estimated that the steam feed will increase the cutting capacity at least 8%, as it does away with the old rope system, which caused frequent and expensive delays by breaking. The steam is applied direct to the carriage, which answers the lever much more quickly, and with greater precision than the old system. It's the steam nigger, which is under the control of the sawyer, by the more rapid handling of the log, and the turning or canting but once instead of twice, as by the old method, will increase the capacity of the mill another 8%.

The series of iron live rollers, 40 feet long, has been added to the 44 feet already in the mill, making 84 feet in all. Over these the slabs and edgings are carried to a point opposite the slab slasher, where they are picked up by conveyor chains and transferred to the table, cut up into 4 foot lengths, carried on over the table by the same chains, and dumped into the shoot. Here, the slabs suitable for cutting into lath are picked out as they pass the lath mill, and the remainder carried away by the large refuse conveyor chain. The above improvements were put in by the D. J. Murray Manufacturing Company of Wausau, Wisconsin.

A new re-saw, Fischer's patent, of Chicago, of greater capacity than those now in use, will replace one of the old machines. A new trimmer and edger of late pattern will be put in, for the purpose of trimming and edging such lumber as may need it, after passing through the re-saws.

As is well known, Captain Pike is progressive in his ideas, and is always on the look for the best and latest improvements for his mill. In addition to the new machinery mentioned above, all machines heretofore in use are undergoing a thorough overhauling, and will be in perfect shape when the time comes to blow the first whistle in the spring – which is a signal for renewed activity that causes a feeling of gladness to all.

The mill will run night and day and will give employment to a large number of men and boys, probably not less than 150. The captain has his own electric light plant, of 116 candlepower lamp capacity, and it will require the full complement of lamps to light the mill and yard for the night run. The cut for the year will be at least 20,000,000 feet, and the mill will be in shape to begin at the earliest possible moment after the ice goes out. The new dock begun last year will be extended 600 feet more, giving piling room for over 20,000,000 feet. To give an idea of what this means, the cuts of 1889 represent over one fourth million dollars in lumber and will bring into Bayfield this amount.

"When Something Is Gained, Something Is Lost"

Lillian Tate-Wilkinson, daughter of Bayfield pioneers, Andrew and Nellie Tate, in a message to the Bayfield Women's Club gathering, March 24th 1904 summarizes the annihilated status and plight of the New Wisconsin's timber industry.

Said Mrs. Wilkinson: "The first steamer to visit Bayfield was the *Lady Elgin*, June 16, 1856. She was lost on Lake Michigan with 600 excursionists from Milwaukee on board in 1860. This steamer brought the engineer and carpenters to build the mill. On July 27, the *Mineral Rock* arrived bringing the engine and other machinery for the mill and also one of the owners, John T. Caho. The mill was built about where Captain Pike's mill now stands near the foot of Broad Street, and was finished and began sawing in September, 1856, and thus began the industry that was to rob Wisconsin of her grand forests, and put millions of dollars into the pockets of the lumberman. It is very hard for us to realize that the shores were ever covered with thick forests."

R. D. Pike Saw Mill
BHA Pike Research Center Archive Collection

The above picture is that of the third saw mill constructed in Bayfield. The first mill that was built in Bayfield was in 1856 by John T. Caho who relocated from Washington DC area. It was destroyed by fire January 12, 1857. The second mill was built by the same company, and in the early 1860s sold to Samuel Stewart Vaughn, who after running it a few years dismantled it and moved it to Ashland. In 1868 Captain R.D. Pike erected the mill shown above on the site of his present plant. The capacity of this mill was 10,000 feet per day and was considered a model structure. *Bayfield County Press*, January 1, 1903

Henry J. Wachsmuth Lumber Company Mill Circa 1920
BHA Pike Research Center Archive Collection

Bayfield's Big Mills Still Lumbering

By Editor- W. H. Holmes

Bayfield Progress - July 1, 1909

Captain R.D. Pike died on March 27, 1906 and from there the family moved from the Bayfield Peninsula area westward. In the spring of 1904, the Captain sold his business, lock, stock and barrel, to Henry J. Wachsmuth. Brilliance as a businessman favored him forward politically in the scheme of local governance where he served as alderman and Mayor of Bayfield for many years. The *Progress* now provides further insight into the man who became lumber king of the Bayfield peninsula for near twenty years until the sweet music of the mill's steam whistle gasped the last breath in the fall 1927.

The *Progress* man has been so long laboring with pencil among the potato fields of central Wisconsin, that he scarcely realized that there was much lumbering left in northern Wisconsin. But since coming to Bayfield he has found that he was mistaken. There's still lots of hemlock, birch, maple, cedar and some pine left in our end of the county, the Apostle Islands and places on the South Shore of Lake Superior that furnishes work for lumbermen during the winter months.

The mills supplied are two in Ashland, one in Washburn and three in Bayfield, which includes the Wachsmuth Lumber Company, the Bayfield Mill Company at Roy's Point, and the Red Cliff Lumber Company.

We dropped in on the hustlers at the mill in this city at 5 p.m. one day last week and took a look at the bee hive of the industry, where the band saws were sawing planks and boards at a lively rate while the two log carriages, each with its quota of experts were riding back and forth, having "nothing to do" only to see that the auto lumber carriage did the work satisfactory; and a man with a stick full of figures measured the end of every log as it was brought up automatically from the big pond in the rear of the mill.

As the lumber is delivered on the carriers as fast as sawed, another man keeps tally of the exact amount of boards measured in feet they have produced and in less time than it takes to tell it, the boards and slabs go hustling along automatically by a system of chain belts which propel the carriers, with men standing at the proper place to start the boards and slabs on their destination.

Waterfront Tramway on South 2nd Street Circa 1906
BHA Pike Research Center Archive Collection
RJN-BH-31

What is good of the slab after it reaches the basement finds its way to the lath mill, and what is only fit for wood is sawed the proper length and taken in a dump cart to the wood piles covering a large space in the yards. Some of which is burned at the mill, and much finding ready sale in the city.

But returning to the lumber, after it leaves the mill from its automatic delivery chain carriage, it reaches the hands of men who put it on the tramway cars, when a man with a horse trundles the little cars of lumber out in the vicinity of the big slips and docks, where the product is piled in a systematic manner ready for and shipping either by boats, barges or by rail.

Other features about the big plant are a large shingle mill, also a big blacksmith and machine shop for the repair of their machinery. The big band saws have to be changed two or three times daily, giving work to several men in the filing department. The motive power of this mill as well as all others of its class on the bay is from powerful engines, fed by the sawdust and trimmings from the mill. There is also at this mill a complete electric lighting plant of over 300 lights, as the business runs day and night with complete shifts of men to the number of one hundred twenty-five for each shift in all departments when running to its full capacity.

Kurz Downey Box Factory
BHA Pike Research Center Archive Collection

Mr. Henry J. Wachsmuth is manager of this concern. The book keeping and office work is under the supervision of Mr. John B. Bovee. Everything moves off on the business end, like the mill, all "OK." The pay-roll of the Wachsmuth Lumber Company averages about $15,000.00 monthly and the two other mills mentioned about as much or more. The majority of the men from the three mills last mentioned make Bayfield headquarters for disbursing and spending a large share of about $30,000.00 monthly in wages in Bayfield from lumber manufacturing alone, for seven months in the year. For months during the winter nearly as much in monthly wages is paid out for preparing the logs for the following season's mill work.

And it is said by expert lumbermen that in this county and vicinity which includes the islands, it will take at least ten years longer to exhaust the supply of workable logs into lumber. So, if Bayfield profits by the sad experience of many other places and hustles to get the farms under way with fruits and diversified farming, they will not experience the deadness of a collapse when the mills stop, for they will have other industries going and a busy lot of workers on the rich lands. Various towns of the country are making rapid progress and everybody is happy to see the new change as they were sorry to see the old order of things go. And from what we have seen the actual transition has commenced. It is apparently slow, but sure.

Another institution not to be forgotten running practically in connection and alongside of the Wachsmuth Lumber Company's plant, but under entire different management is Bayfield Lumber & Fuel Company, which does an up-to-date planing mill business, doors, sash, screen doors, mill work-etc. Mr. Carl Johnson is the owner and manager and Mary McNeal book keeper. They have an up-to-date mill, well equipped with everything needful in machinery.

The box factory of the *Kurz-Downey Company* of Chicago which will soon be in operation, will give employment to two or three hundred people. It has been in operation a year and they will stay by us many years after the big mills are gone, to work up as much timber that the farmers can spare when clearing their farms.

The Kurz-Downey Company factory burned to the ground on November 11, 1910. The factory was located at the site where William Knight previously operated a saw mill on Roy's Point, near to two miles north of Bayfield, Wisconsin.

Roy's Point Mill
Willam Knight's sawmill on Roy'd Point
RJN-BH-85

Bayfield's Eastern Waterfront Lumber Dock Circa 1906
Steamer *Ireland* loads Railroad Ties and Dimensional Lumber

RJN-BH-123

End of an Era

By Melvin R. Clark

Mel Clark was born on November 4, 1912 and graduated from Bayfield's old Abraham Lincoln High School in 1932. The Clark family hailed from Two Rivers, Wisconsin and arrived in Bayfield by train in August of 1915. Furniture and all their worldly possessions followed in a freight car. Father Oliver Clark, a carpenter and home builder by trade, eventually became one of the Township of Bayfield's earlier rural route postmen.

This short story relays the last days of the Wachsmuth Lumber Company is transcribed from a hand-typed booklet titled *Growing up in Bayfield, Wisconsin*. This forty-five page biography offered eleven descriptions of life in the Township and Village of Bayfield of which the following essay is one. The booklet was dedicated it to Mr. Clark's "members of my family and to my friends." No date is offered but it may safely be assumed Mr. Clark was in the mid to latter stages of life. Mr. Clark's rendition of the final days of the Wachsmuth Lumber Company and there-by lumbering in the Bayfield peninsula in general is hereby presented. Mel Clark now provides the following information:

The Wachsmuth saw mill was the largest industry in Bayfield, employing many of the men in the area. It was started by Mr. Pike in the late 19th century and was later owned by Mr. Henry J. Wachsmuth. From our home [area of 225 South Fifth Street] we could see most of the mill buildings located below in the mill yard.

Most of the logs came to the mill by rail or boat. The railroad hauled the logs to the saw mill site. A tugboat and scow would bring in large load of logs from the islands. Most of the logs were put in the mill pond and were later prepared for the mill. This scow or barge was a large wooden boat with a flat bottom. And one end was the steam engine and the operator's room. From his position, he could see the entire area. A large swivel-mounted boom extended from his location to about amidships, where it was attached to a large clam, a machine which could grasp logs and move them. The operator, with various levers could lift and turn the clam, could open and close the jaws, and place the logs to any desired position. Several logs could be unloaded together into the water with this equipment. A number of large logs chained together, also called a boom, and was placed near the mill pond to prevent the logs from floating away. The tugboat would then tow the empty scow back to the lumber camp on the island for a new load.

Steaming Away
Lake Superior Towing Company's *"Bayfield"*

James and Marge Miller Family Collection

When the logs had soaked in the mill pond enough, they were prepared for the saw mill. This was done by two men, one on each end of a log. They were called "skinners" and wore special shoes with steel cleats for safety on the slippery logs and short pants to prevent getting wet. The tools they used to remove loose bark and knots were an adz, a cutting tool with a thin arched blade set at right angles to the handle, and a short pike pole, a wooden shaft with a pointed steel head. When the logs were ready, they were taken to the conveyor, which pulled the log up to the second floor where it was rolled onto a machine called a carriage, operated by steam. The operator, the sawyer, sat near the front and worked the levers which adjusted the logs to receive the desired cut. The large endless steel band saw with large cutting teeth was located on the ground floor near its steam-driven engine. It passed over a wooden pulley then extended to a similar wooden pulley on the second floor, where it was lined up with the carriage. When the log was positioned for the cut, the carriage would move forward to bring the log in contact with the saw blade. When the logs were cut, the carriage would return the log for the next cut. The sawyer's work required a lot of skill and was a dangerous operation. The boards cut from the logs were sent to smaller saws where the ends were trimmed to the desired length.

Cedar boards went to the shingle mill, where they were cut and shaped to make roof shingles, packed in a bundle called a square. The lath mill cut thin strips of wood used in building houses. The laths were fastened to the building studs to hold the plaster in place for construction. The slab and trimmings were sold as firewood, sent to the burner, or used as fuel for the boilers. The cut boards were inspected and separated according to quality. Those that were free of knots, splits, or cracks were sent to the planing mill for processing. This was a separate and noisy place where the boards were sent through a large lathe with sharp cutters to make a smooth finish on all four sides. The finished lumber was stacked up to air dry to be used in the building industry.

Waiting for the Scow *Badger*
Lake Superior Towing Company's "Henry W"

James and Marge Miller Family Collection

Lake Superior Towing Company's scow *Badger* Circa 1915
BHA Pike Research Center Archive Collection

The curled up shavings, called excelsior, were packed in containers and were sold to companies that had uses for it, like packaging. The sawdust was picked up from the floor by a large vacuum and blower mounted on the roof. It was then blown outside through a large pipe into a huge pile. The sawdust was sold to fishermen who had ice houses and to farmers and builders for insulation and for keeping ice.

The constant use of the band saw blade and the blade's of other saws make sharpening a necessity. The band saw was removed from its fastening, rolled up, and sent to the filing shop where there was equipment for that work. The dull blades or tools needing sharpening were clamped in a vice which held an item securely while being worked on. Long handled mill files were used for sharpening. This was another kind of work that required a great deal of skill. The workmen were known as filers, a most desirable trade, which paid a high wage.

A tramway system, consisting of an elevated wood structure, extended the length of the mill yard, including access to several docks or slips, as they were called. It was built to haul small cars loaded with lumber. The cars ran on small steel rails with suitable switches. The cars were loaded with rough, green boards at the saw mill and pulled by a horse to the proper area. The lumber was then piled in criss-cross fashion to air dry. The tramway was extended to the surrounding docks where the lumber could be stacked. Large lumber carrying boats could load the lumber into their holds to take to the ports along the Great Lakes to supply the high demand for the wood for buildings and furniture.

We played with the tram cars when the mill was not operating. It was like a small railroad, great fun to push the cars, and then ride for a short distance. I am sure that the workers did not mind looking for the cars on returning to work the next day. On Sunday morning after Sunday school, Harry Hessing and I decided to check out the saw mill tram. It was very quiet at the mill, and we had it all to ourselves, or so it seemed. We were switching the tracks on one of the rails when Harry fell and injured his arm. About this time, Mr. Egan, the watchmen, appeared on the scene. Harry was crying and I was scared; we were afraid of the watchmen. When he saw we were all right, he said, "You boys get the hell out of here and don't come back again." Needless to say, that ended our fun on the tram.

One summer during school vacation it was decided to have a woodworking class for the boys Sunday school class. Mr. Smith was designated to be the instructor. He was a young man who served as the church assistant in other activities. Our shop would be in the church kitchen. Our first class was a tour of the saw mill, very interesting and informative. When the tour was over, we were given some boards that could be used in our class. The pieces were smooth and easily cut with our class saws. We were taught how to cut and fit the parts of a birdhouse, and how to sand them and assemble them. They were later painted in different colors. This was a good project and we all learned a great deal about wood and its uses. We learned to build items by ourselves, and applied this training and manual training classes in school.

When the forest trees were cut and used in this area, there was no raw material for the mill. The Wachsmuth saw mill and lumber company shut down completely during the late summer of 1927. This was a devastating time for Bayfield, with the loss of work for so many. Our home on Fifth Street was on the bluff above the mill. From the vantage point on our front porch, we watched the closing of the saw mill as to begin with the removal of the burner. This was a tall steel structure with a rounded dome covered with steel wire mesh to contain sparks and embers while allowing the smoke to pass through. The base had several large doors to where the bark and slabs of unwanted wood scraps were burned. It was also used to supply some heat for the steam boilers. On the scheduled date, the dynamite, which has been placed in the base, was set off causing a tremendous noise. The huge burner toppled and crashed to the ground. A large cloud of dust erupted from the explosion.

The steam-operated work whistle was tied down and continued to blast until it ran out of steam for a final farewell to the end of an era.

Unloading "Silver-Sided" Herring
BHA Pike Research Center Archive Collection

The Commercial Fishing Industry of 1886

By Superintendent of Wisconsin Fisheries- James Nevin

Bayfield Progress – Reprinted February 6, 1911

The following descriptor of the Harbor City commercial fishing industry is communicated from the *Annual Report of the Commissioners of Fish and Fisheries for 1887*, by Superintendent of Fisheries- James Nevin, Wisconsin Conservation Commission. This synopsis was intended to provide general informational features for then Governor of Wisconsin- Jeremiah Rusk, State Legislators, and especially the board members of the Wisconsin Fishery Commission, presently Wisconsin Department of Natural Resources. Appointed to the fishery commission at the time from the Village of Bayfield was Currie G. Bell. Remaining members included Edwin E. Bryant, Calvert Spensley, James J. Hogan, William J. Starr, and Henry D. Smith.

Description of Bayfield Fisheries: Owing to its excellent location in the immediate vicinity of the excellent fishing grounds, Bayfield for quite a number of years has been largely interested in fishing, and the fisheries occupy the attention of a majority of the citizens. According to the estimates of Mr. Frank Boutin, twenty-five percent of those engaged in the fishery are Chippewa Indian, and the remainders are chiefly Canadians and American. Of late years and to date, the majority of the fishermen are Norwegian and Swedish Americans.

The fisheries are persecuted during the entire year, although there is little activity in the winter. The season practically opens with the first breaking up of the ice in spring, when the gill net fishermen, who were formerly the most numerous classes, begin catching whitefish and trout among the Apostle Islands and the shores of the mainland both east and west. By the middle or last of May many of these, with a large number of additional men, begin setting pound nets about the islands and along the main shore for a distance of nearly one hundred miles. The number of nets has increased annually until Bayfield has become the center of one of the most important pound net fisheries on the whole chain of lakes. By the last of July the greater part of the pound net fishing is over, and one after another the nets are removed, the fishermen again starting out with gill nets. By the first of October all of the pound nets have been taken out and gill net fishing occupies the attention of majority of the people.

Shipments and Preparation of Bayfield Fishery Products: Until recently almost the entire catch from both pound nets and gill nets were salted and shipped to other towns on the lakes, including Chicago, Detroit, Cleveland and Buffalo. No fresh fish were shipped prior to 1876, but from that date until 1883, a small quantity was shipped annually.

The introduction of the fish collecting, the fish tug *N. Boutin*, and building of the railroad gave an impetus to this industry, and in the spring of 1884 a second steamer was purchased. An important trade in fresh fish was soon developed. During the year 1884, about sixty tons were shipped, nearly all of which went to St. Paul and Minneapolis. The quantity of salt fish shipped during the same year was thirteen thousand half-barrels.

The succeeding season the fresh fish trade was much more extensive, and what otherwise would have been salted was packed in ice and sent into the interior, chiefly to St. Paul and Minneapolis. No smoked fish have been put up in the village for shipment, the business being confined wholly to a few smoked by the Indians and other fishermen for family use. About thirty barrels of oil were made by the pound net fishermen is 1884; no caviar has been prepared since 1878, when Hart Pincus came to Bayfield for that purpose. After remaining about two months he became discouraged and left the place, taking with him 750 pounds of caviar put up during his stay.

Statistics of Fisheries: In 1885 there were one hundred and eighty-two men engaged in fishing, twenty-seven others in collecting, preparing, and shipping of fish, and six others in making barrels and boats, for the fish trade. These, including their families, make a total of six hundred and fifteen persons dependent upon the fisheries. If we exclude the twenty pound nets owned by Ashland parties, there were one hundred and twenty-four pond nets owned and operated by Bayfield fishermen in addition to two thousand gill nets and eight seines. The total production of the Bayfield fisheries was 640,000 pounds of fresh fish, and 2,192,000 pounds of salt fish, with a total value of $60,080.

Bayfield Fish Trade: Two steamers were employed in collecting the fish, one of these fishing for several months in the fall. There were also two schooners engaged in transporting the nets to and from the fishing grounds, in supplying slats and barrels to the camps, and bringing back cargoes of salt fish. Three firms, Boutin & Mahan, Rich and Atwood, and Frank Boutin, each had an extensive fishing business, the former two handling both fresh and salt fish.

These parties control the entire catch of the Bayfield fishermen and all of the salt fish of Ashland, sending their tugs and sailboats for a distance of thirty or forty miles westward, and fifty to sixty miles along the eastern shore. They handled in 1885 over 600,000 pounds of fresh and frozen fish, and upwards of 22,000 half barrels of salt fish. The firms furnish barrels and salt, delivering them at the fishing stations to be filled, and freighting the catch to the town.

Gill Net Fishing in Open Waters: The following account of the gill net and pound fishing is largely obtained from information kindly furnished by Messrs. Nelson Boutin and J. W. Atwood. Prior to 1870, when Mr. Boutin came to the region, there had been three or four crews of gill net fishermen, in addition to the Indians that fished for home supply. From that time the gill net fishery gradually increased until about 1883, when it began to be superseded by the pound nets. In 1885 there were about fifteen crews that fished gill nets exclusively, and twenty-seven others that were in interested in both gill nets and pound nets fisheries.

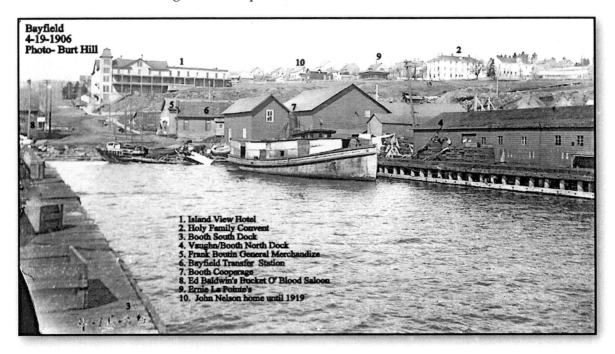

Bayfield
4-19-1906
Photo- Burt Hill

1. Island View Hotel
2. Holy Family Convent
3. Booth South Dock
4. Vaughn/Booth North Dock
5. Frank Boutin General Merchandize
6. Bayfield Transfer Station
7. Booth Cooperage
8. Ed Baldwin's Bucket O' Blood Saloon
9. Ernie La Pointe's
10. John Nelson home until 1919

Washington Avenue Beachhead Circa 1899
RJN-BH-02

The season opens about the 1st of April and continues until the ice forms and prevents the boats from getting out. In the early spring they fish about the islands, and later along the shore between Bayfield and Carp River, (Marquette County, Michigan) remaining till October when they return to the islands to fish till the close of the season, or, as was frequently the case, proceed to Isle Royale, Michigan and remain there until stormy winter weather drives them home. As many as thirty boats, with a total of seventy-five or eighty Bayfield fishermen, visited the Island Royale grounds in the fall of 1883, and twenty boats were there in 1884, but as they met with poor success the latter year very few made the trip in 1885.

Three men ordinarily constitute a crew for gill net fishing, but at least one-third of the boats carry only two. They average from forty to eighty nets to the boat. A few of the boats have nets made of fine twine for spring fishing and coarser ones for the trout fishing in the fall. This is especially true of those visiting Isle Royale, but most of those fishing along the southern shore and among the islands have only one set. The nets are 65 fathoms long, and vary from 4 ½ to 5 ½ inches in mesh size. Some of them are rigged like the old-fashioned Lake Michigan nets, with stones and floats, and the others in the more modern style with leads and corks. Fifteen or twenty nets constitute a gang, each crew usually having four gangs, and keeping three in the water at one time. The boats are mostly mackinaws, and smaller than those of Duluth. They are worth about one hundred dollars each. In former years it is estimated that the average gill net crew caught between four hundred and five hundred half barrels for a year's fishing, but in 1884 did not exceed three hundred barrels to the boat. In 1885 it was much better, and is estimated at five hundred half barrels.

Gill Net fishing Through the Ice: The ice fishing with gill nets varies considerably from year to year. It ordinarily begins early in January and lasts for six, eight or even ten weeks. Two or three men constitute a crew, running from forty to fifty nets. These are set in lines of four nets each, at right angles to the shore; the gangs are half a mile apart and left in the water four or five days before hauling. Only fine nets are used. The sediment would collect too readily on coarse twine, making the nets more noticeable and keeping the fish away. One crew of men ordinarily secures an average of three hundred pounds of fish daily, working about four days in a week. The marketable catch is about one-half trout and one-half whitefish. In addition quantities of suckers and lawyers are commonly thrown away. Some of the crew has small canvas tents or huts with stoves, and they move them from hole to hole on the ice, thus protecting them from the winter cold. Others have horses and sleighs for visiting their nets, driving to and from the fishing grounds, while others still are obliged to go it afoot and work without shelter, and of course, can fish only during moderate weather. Some years, from twenty to twenty-five crews are engaged in net fishing through the ice. During the winter of 1884-1885 only about ten crews were thus employed, and some of these fished only a short time.

Pound Net Fishery: The first pound net set in Bayfield was by Mr. Boutin, who came here from Ashland in the spring of 1871. The industry was not important until about 1880. Several new nets were purchased in that year, and in 1883 the number had reached twenty-five or thirty, exclusive of those owned by Ashland fishermen. In 1884 not less than eighty new ones were employed, and in 1885 ten or twelve more were added. They are set in water varying from twelve to sixty feet in depth, the deepest ones in 1885 being only about forty feet; but one of the dealers intended making and setting a seventy-five foot net that fall. The nets are of the ordinary pattern, with forty to eighty rods leaders of six inch mesh, a heart of 5 inch mesh, and usually a 28 foot pot of 3-inch mesh. They are provided with tunnels ten feet square at the mouth, sixteen feet long, and having an inner opening of two by six feet. The nets are usually set between the 15th of May and 1st of June. Some of the men fish gill nets before the season opens, and a few continue to fish them in connection with the pound nets. Most of the fishing is over by the first of August, and half of the nets are taken out. The remainder fish until the last of September, when the fishermen fit out for the gill net fishing. Of late there has been a tendency to prolong the pound net season, and on September 5, 1885, fully half of the nets were still in the water.

In 1884, for the first time a pound net was fished in winter, and, though not successful, there was a growing inclination to set them during the spawning season for the whitefish. It seems probable that within a comparatively short time a majority of the nets will be fished in fall and early winter, as well as other seasons.

The nets are generally purchased from the dealers, some of the fishermen paying cash, but a greater number getting them on credit and paying for them in fish. A few however are owned by dealers and other capitalists. These are fished on shares, the net taking from two-fifths to one-half of the catch. Three fishermen usually constitute a crew, fishing from four to five nets, and where more nets are worked additional men are required. The fishermen set their nets about the islands in shallow waters near sandy beaches and bays along the main shore, building shanties nearby where they camp during the season, and are visited regularly by the collecting boats, which take their fish and furnish them with supplies and provisions.

The dealers estimate the average catch for each pound net fished in 1884 at 125 barrels or about $200.00. The marketable catch averages 90% whitefish, .07% trout, and .03% sturgeon in addition to considerable quantities of small whitefish. A good many of the sturgeon are thrown away. Mr. Boutin thought that the catch of 1885 would be more than a quarter that of the previous year. This small yield he believed in no way indicated a scarcity of fish, but was accounted for by the fish remaining in deeper water, where the gill nets have caught larger quantities than usual. The heavy thunderstorms during the pound net season may have had a decided influence in keeping the fish out of the shoaler water.

Seine Fishery: The seining of fish began about 1899, with small seines 300 to 485 feet in length and 12 to 18 feet deep. They are hauled during the four or five weeks between the 5th of June and middle of July. The catch is principally whitefish, though considerable quantities of herring are also taken, but, owing to the small demand, few are saved. The fishing at present is chiefly in the vicinity of Bark Bay Point and Sand River, along the western boundary of the Bayfield peninsula. The fishermen seldom make blind hauls, as other places, but have a man on the lookout on some elevated point of land to watch for fish, and when a school is seen it is surrounded by the seine and hauled ashore. The average catch is estimated at about 100 barrels of salt fish. Thought formerly, it is said to have been three times that quantity. In 1885 there were 13 seines owned in Bayfield, but only eight or ten of them were fished to any extent during the season, and the catch, owing to the absence of the fish from the shore waters, was unusually light.

Hand-Line Fishing through the Ice: There is considerable hand line fishing, or "bobbing" as it is locally called by the Indians and others, through the ice in winter. The former take fish for their own use, but a few of the whites make it a business, freezing their catch and selling to Duluth dealers. The catch is usually small, but sometimes a man will get three hundred to four hundred pounds in a day.

Spearing: In the morning each "bob" fisherman provides himself with herring enough to serve as bait for the day's fishing by means of a little homemade wire spear used through a hole in the ice. The spearing of trout through the ice by the Indians is quite common in certain localities. They usually have a brilliantly painted decoy resembling a fish, which they dart into the water through an opening in the ice, and the trout are attracted toward it and speared.

Other Fisheries: No Trammel nets have been fished in the locality, and Fyke nets have been employed in only one instance, this being in the spring of 1884, when a small number were fished at the mouth of one of the large streams without success."

Mr. Nevin says: "During the year of 1890, 478,632 pounds of lake trout were caught at Bayfield and for which the fishermen received an average price of 2.8 cent per pound, or a total of $12,501.09. In 1884 the price paid to the fishermen for filling was: $3.50-$4.00 per half barrel for Number 1 and Number 2 whitefish; $1.50-$1.75 for Number 3 whitefish; $2.50-$3.00 for trout and Siskowit; $1.50

for sturgeon; $1.00-$1.50 for herring; $2.00 for pike; and $1.25 for suckers. In 1885 the price was somewhat less.

In 1909, the catch was 429,235 pounds, for which the average market price was 6.5 cents per pound, yielding a total of $27,885.87. While the intervening years show a decline of but 49,397 pounds in the catch of siskowit and lake trout, the market value shows an increase of over 100 per cent, amounting to $15,383.58.

In 1890 the catch of whitefish was 986,962 as compared with 25,494 pounds in 1909, and which indicated that the waters of Lake Superior have been practically depleted of this fish. The supply of lake trout was maintained and increased by the planting of fry of that species. There is no question that if whitefish propagation and been followed as extensively as that of lake trout, the decline of whitefish would have been no more pronounced than that of lake trout.

During the months of March and April of the years 1886 and 1887, the Commission of Fisheries shipped in baggage cars from the Milwaukee hatchery some ten million of what was called "bluefin whitefish." These fish were planted in Chequamegon Bay, out from Ashland, and to plant them we were compelled to cut holes through the ice. Hawley Brothers, of Ontonogon, Michigan, wrote and condemned me for planting this species of fish in Lake Superior waters. In 1890 fishermen began to find the mature fish in their nets, and in 1899 they caught 425,000 pounds, the value of which was $11,317.00. In 1903 they caught 2, 038, 522 pounds of the fish and marketed them for $61,782.00. During the last five years very few have been caught and this year, none have been reported. At the present time, it looks as though the Lake Superior waters have been entirely depleted of the bluefin. Twenty years ago fifty percent of the lake trout caught were of the siskowit variety. Now the proportion is hardly one to five hundred of the regular variety caught, and which is accounted for in that the Commission of Fisheries has not been propagating the siskowit.

The fish hatchery, situated as it is at Bayfield, is the backbone of one of the most important industries in the vicinity. I do not believe that there is another department or institution supported by the state that yields such generous returns to the community at large as that of the Commissioners of Fisheries. All classes of people, rich and poor, share in the benefits derived from the work.

Fishermen Mending Nets at Booth Fisheries, January 20, 1905
BHA Pike Research Center Archive Collection
Courtesy Apostle Islands Historical Preservation Conservancy

The Tug *F. R. Anderson*
A Day's Herring Catch

Alfred Booth Packing Company Dock: Circa 1900

Robert J. Nelson Collection

The Herring Fishers

Bayfield County Press - Saturday, December 10, 1898

The young Scandinavians to which the article will allude, one of which may have been the author's grandfather Johannes Nelson who arrived to America in 1897, spoke to his son Julian B. Nelson in the early 1930s that the tugs, like the *R.W. Currie* and *F.R. Anderson* had no mechanical net lifting apparatus to start with. Rather, the tugs enlisted the use of a roller mechanism attached to the bow of the boat, over which, the nets, loaded with fish were pulled on to the deck by hand. Three to four men would fill the bow area first, then would "grab an armful" and walk back to the port and starboard sides with up to 15 tons of the prized product. Nelson said his father mentioned to him how ornery the fish pilers would become if the captain was not paying attention to keeping the nets directly alongside the tug's bow, because if the winds caused the tug to drift side-ways in the trough of the seas, the nets would to spill back into the lake.

A Night on the Dark Waters of Lake Superior and *the Fisherman's Life Not a Continual Picnic, but He Is Satisfied If the Fish Are Plentiful* were the subtitles on this date. This poem, without an author designate, begins and concludes this critique of life as a herring fisherman on the icy waters of Lake Superior.

> *Three fishers went sailing way to the west-*
> *Away to the west as the sun went down;*
> *Each thought on the moment who loved him the best,*
> *And the children stood watching them out of town;*
> *For the men must work young women must weep*
> *And there's little to earn and many to keep*
> *Though the harbor bar be moaning.*

People whose only interest in the finny tribe is centered on the delicious piece of baked whitefish or trout served up for dinner or the boiled herring for breakfast perhaps understand very little of the process by which the fish has been secured for their enjoyment. Even the sportsman, who, seated on the sunny bank of the stream, or floating lazily over the placid surface of one or more inland lakes in a rowboat, beguiles the dwellers in the water to leave their home and grace a string of beauties he holds up for a photograph, may know little about labor and excitement incident to fishing as a business on the open waters of the great lakes. There is little of the romantic connected with it, but much of hard work, exposure to all kinds of weather and the facing of danger falls to the lot of the fisherman.

The methods of fishing have not greatly changed as far as taking the fish is concerned for hundreds of years, but great improvements have been made by which greater numbers are taken in the same length of time. Within the recollection of people of the present generation most of the work was done by fishermen who lived at various points along the shores of the lakes, some of them, perhaps, many miles from a port. Every afternoon the fisherman and his one or two helpers went out to the fishing grounds in his Mackinaw boat, a craft indigenous to the lakes both in build and rig, and after setting the nets, returned to the shore to wait till morning, when he again went to raise the nets. After several catches have been made he loaded his craft and sailed or rowed to the nearest port and sold his fish or shipped them to some large market like Chicago or Milwaukee; in the latter case, sometimes to be swindled by fraudulent inspectors or commission merchants.

But times have changed, and the old way was to slow for the present. The A. Booth Packing Company, with markets all over the Union and in parts of Canada, control nearly the whole business, and the system has been remodeled. The Mackinaw boats are not all gone, but there are not so many, and one steam tug does the work of a large number of this little sailing craft.

During most of the season the men are engaged in taking whitefish and trout, but as the cold weather comes on and the closed season for the big fish begins, they turn their attention to the herring, and every available spot on the docks is covered with a temporary house for dressing and packing the small and delicious fish. In the work of catching, dressing and packing the herring about thirty-five men have been employed. The crews who do the catching and own their outfit are furnished the use of a tug. They received for their fish $.40 per hundred pounds. They so arrange the work that the men who put in one night on the fishing grounds spend the next on shore, and also help through the next day to dress the fish.

The writer a few days ago went out with the *Currie*, the tug used in this branch of the business, to get an idea of the work from personal observation. The time set out for going is 3 p.m., but the crew is not all there promptly. They begin to string along and get the nets and other parts of the outfit aboard. About 3:50 lines are cast-off in the boat is steaming for Chebomnicon [Chequamegon] Bay, a few miles to the southeast, on the southern side of Madeline Island. There is a fresh breeze from the southwest and the air is full of snow. There is a little swell on the water, and occasionally the spray breaks over the bow of the tug, but there is no apparent danger to excite anyone. A big field of floating ice from Ashland's bay is encountered near the Point and the boat stops, but the ice proves to be broken into small pieces and the engineer is signaled "full speed ahead." In a little more than an hour from Bayfield, after winding about the devious course of the South Channel, the *Currie* stops at a point about a half-mile off shore and the setting [of small mesh nets] begins.

The nets, neatly folded in trays, are given a bath of hot water to thaw them out. The night air blowing over the bosom of Lake Superior during the last week in November is not very warm, and even a heavy overcoat will not keep an idler from growing chilly. The water freezes on the deck, making it slippery, but the men keep at their work with as little concern as if standing in spiked baseball shoes on terra firma, instead of walking upon the few square feet on the after deck of a rolling tug and within a short distance of the icy waters of Lake superior, ready to receive the one making a misstep.

A lantern is lashed to the top of the buoy, a long line fastened to the bottom, and the buoy cast overboard. The nets are slowly payed out, the weights on one side sinking them to the bottom of the lake, 22 fathoms down, and the floats on the other side of the net holding them in an upright position. The engineer is signaled to go ahead slow, and all is well until a tangle is found in the nets, when someone suddenly shouts, "stop" then perhaps "backup." In this way the tug moves slowly along for 2 miles. When the last net is reeled off another buoy is set in the same manner as the first. These stops and starts severely test the patience of the engineer, and they are quite frequent, but Briggs seemed to be quite as pleasant at the finish as the start.

In order to commence lifting with the boat bow to leeward, she runs back to the first buoy and the anchor is cast. The crew gets off their oilers and climbs down into the cabin. It's a little after six o'clock and the lunches are spread out on the table. Hot coffee is served all around, and these men may lay in the hold and eat as if they were hungry, while the waves outside dash against the boat and there is a rising and falling motion of the stern, with which the stomachs of most landlubbers would keep perfect time.

Most of the men have lived on the water since they were big enough to reach any tiller or handle a rope. Captain Nogglegard and several of the crew are Scandinavians, as also are most of the men engaged in the fishing business at this point. Some of them served their apprenticeship on the salt waters of northwestern Europe, from whence come, as a class, it is said, the best sailors in the world. Lake Superior, however, tests their training to the utmost, for the sailors from the Atlantic tell us that it is harder to navigate a boat over the short, choppy seas of the Great Lakes than over the long swells of the ocean. All of the fishermen are strong healthy men, and they need to be such, for the life they follow would either toughen, or kill any man.

Lunch is over, and the fishers smoke, tell stories and chaff one another till they get sleepy, when they light down for a nap in the famous cradle of the seafaring man. Forward, in the engine room, the engineer, too, is trying to snooze. The fire is banked and the steam goes down gradually. Nobody seems to be alive but for the newspaperman, and the only sound to be heard is the hissing of steam, the breaking of the waves, and the dismal bellow of the fog whistle on Chequamegon point. The snow ceases falling and the moon comes out, but soon hides again. How slowly the hands of the clock in the engine room seem to move! Nine o'clock comes at last and the musical whistle of the *Currie* awakens the sleepers, who are soon out and getting into their oilskins again.

The anchor is pulled and, as the tug moves slowly head, the men raise the nets. These fish are a scattering at first and, "ain't going to have a very big haul," and "guess we'll have to wait out here till morning next time" are some of the comments from the crew. But over on the "for-d" deck the fish are being heaped up, and the work grows more exciting as the nets come over the side filled with the little fellows, occasionally squeaking a protest at leaving their native element. After a time nearly all of the space forward of the wheelhouse is stacked up with a squirming mass of fish on the deck and the port side engine room deck is filled up until the tug lists over 20°, when the men make another tack and fill the starboard side. The last buoy is hauled up and the tug steams homeward, arriving at Bayfield at 1:30 with her load. The reader queries "How many pounds in the load?" Would you dare to offer 10,000 pounds as a guess? Too small. This load is not computed by pounds. There are 11 tons, and this is not the best catch of the season.

The trip by the writer was one of the pleasant ones. Another afternoon comes. The storm signal is flying as the tug goes out - but that flag is set to warn the captains of the big steamers, not the fishing crew of a little tug. The wind is from the northwest and quite a sea is rolling in the bay. It snows a little and the temperature is falling. The crew knows they are playing with fate, but they have been taught to laugh at danger, and it means a few more dollars if they win. They reach the fishing grounds where the water is more tranquil, but is snowing so hard that the pilot can hardly see to proceed, and the air is so cold that the crew, toughened as they are, suffers severely while setting the nets.

They anchor and wait for the nets to fill. The wind suddenly shifts to the northeast and in an hour heavy seas are furiously tossing the little boat, but the crew is anxious to save their nets and get a few more fish. Before the usual time they begin to lift. Despite the efforts of the two men at the wheel to hold the boat on her course, she occasionally falls off into the trough of the sea, fouling the nets and throwing the men off their feet. The bow is sheathed with a huge coating of ice and the waves break over the rail, the water rushing on board as it falls. The crew struggles on in this terrible way till the end of the "string" is reached, when the tug makes a rough voyage home, but lands her crew and cargo safely.

This is no overdrawn picture. It has been nearly equaled in the experience of the *Currie*'s crew this season, and escapes like this do not deter them from taking similar risks, but rather encourage them. Sometimes however, the ending of the trip is different. The seas encountered are, perhaps, no worse than on the former trip, but when the boat is laboring so violently to surmount them that the rudder is disabled or the engine breaks down and the merciless waters engulf the craft or sweep her crew onto some reef or shoal. Then, with a few variations to suit the locality, the closing verse of the poem from which we quoted at the beginning becomes applicable.

"Three corpses lay on the shining sands
In the morning gleam as the tide went down,
And the women are weeping and wringing their hands
For those who will never come back to the town,
For men must work and women must weep,
And the sooner it's over the sooner to sleep
And goodbye to the bar and its morning."

Brownstone Loading Operations
BHA Pike Research Center Archive Collection

Quarrying native sandstone around the Bayfield area had a relatively short life of near to thirty years. Early concentration and efforts began on Basswood Island of the Apostle Islands group in 1868. The use of brownstone reached its peak in the 1880s and 1890s when six quarries in the area were supplying eastern markets. Regional quarries, like those at Houghton Point and at R. D. Pike's quarry near Salmo, four miles south of Bayfield, had a much easier go off it transporting their product with the arrival of the railroad in Bayfield in 1883. Popularity of brownstone as an edifice construction product peaked in the 1890s. By 1900 changes in architectural styles and hydraulic cement paved the way for the demise of the industry. The remainder quarries had little long-term impact on Bayfield's economy but the native stone left a lasting heritage i.e. Lincoln High School, Bayfield County Courthouse, Currie Bell building 2nd N. 2nd Street, remain today.

Added insight to quarrying is offered from the *Milwaukee Sentinel* in 1891 and is spinned as only Bayfield's premier promoter, Currie G. Bell could broadcast, "Currie Bell, the well-known editor of Bayfield, is residing at the Plankinton and is on his return home from a sojourn to Madison. The *Sentential* reports Bell speaks to the scribe of Bayfield's brownstone industry near that city: "There are now 10 brownstone quarries in the vicinity of Bayfield, five of them being located on Bass Island and the others near the city. These quarries give employment to nearly 1000 men, and are owned by parties in New York, St. Louis and other cities. The stone used in the brownstone fronts of fashionable New York comes mostly from Connecticut, but is practically the same as that secured around the coast of Lake Superior.

In my opinion the quarrying of sandstone is going to take the place of the pine industry when the woods are stripped." Mr. Bell said. "It is found at various places around the coast of Lake Superior, and they are getting some from the north coast that is almost as hard as granite. It costs a good deal to quarry, but there is some demand I understand. The brownstone quarry in our neighborhood is comparatively soft when first excavated, but grows hard with exposure. The Milwaukee Courthouse is built of it, and you may recollect that there was a good deal of opposition to its use at first, the people thinking it would crumble away. It certainly hasn't done so. There is another virtue of brownstone that is noticeable. It can withstand fire, there being no lime in it. In the "Chicago Fire", the *Chicago Tribune* building, which was built of it, escaped so far as the walls were concerned and they are still in use." *Bayfield County Press* - February 14, 1891

In the Chequamegon Bay area a total of fourteen quarries operating are listed. The two trailing stories affirm solvency and insight into the once viable and speculative business.

Local Peninsula Brownstone Companies: 1870-1900

Milwaukee Sentinel **reprinted in the** *Bayfield County Press* - **February 14, 1891**

- Ashland Brown Stone Company located on Stockton Island; John H. Knight, William Knight, of Bayfield and D. S. Kennedy of Ashland, WI

- Ashland Brown Stone Company; Stockton Island; Bodenschatz, Bodenschatz and Brown of Chicago, IL

- Bass Island Brown Stone Company; Basswood Island; Sweet & Wells of Milwaukee, WI

- Bass Island Brown Stone Company; Basswood Island; French, Lee, Strong & Wells, Chicago, IL and Milwaukee, WI

- Bass Island Brown Stone Co.; Basswood Island—Brooks Leach, & Ritchie, Superior, WI

- Bayfield Brownstone Development Company; Stockton Island & Van Tassel Point, —Denison, Pike & Quayle, Bayfield, WI

- Breckenridge Quarry; Basswood Island—John Breckenridge of Kentucky

- Cook & Hyde; Basswood Island—Cook & Hyde Milwaukee, WI and Minneapolis, MN

- R.D. Pike Quarry; Van Tassel's Point—R.D. Pike, Salmo, WI

- Prentice Brownstone Company; Houghton Point and Hermit Island

- Barr, Ellis, Hamilton, Prentice & Shores; Ashland, WI

- Superior Brownstone Company; Basswood Island; Bailey, Barr & Rogers; Ashland, WI

- Washburn Stone Company; Houghton Point area; Babcock & Smith of Kasota, MN

- Wieland Brothers Quarry; Houghton Falls

Chequamegon Peninsula Brownstone Quarrying

Bayfield County Press - May 24, 1884

From an ancient text book, *Geology of Wisconsin,* 1873-1878, Lake Superior brownstone qualities are articulated. For the reader who is geologically inclined the following review may satisfy academic needs. "The regions sandstone presents itself as a horizontal sandstone base, which varies from deep reddish-brown, through various tinges of red, to fawn color, the red shades being the most common. This sandstone is quite aluminous, carrying usually some feldspathic particles, whose perceptibility as a white alteration has often given rise to a kaolin-like substance, which, in lighter colored varieties, readily substance between the grains. The following analysis is provided by Mr. E. T. Sweet and represents two different sandstones of the Chequamegon region; Basswood Island is 87.02 % Silica, 7.17 % Alumina, 3.91 % Iron peroxide, .11 Limes, .06 Magnesia, 1.43 % Potash, and .22 % soda. The horizontal sandstone of the area is confined to the shores of the lake, whose level has never been observed at a greater height than 370 feet. Next the *Press* scribe visits Captain Pike's sandstone block pit operations located near to four miles south of Bayfield at the old *Omaha* train stop, near Salmo, Wisconsin and relays the following insight.

Bayfield's brownstone business is booming these days. A fact that is particularly gratifying to the *Press,* to which it has persistently advocated, during the past year and a half, is the advisability of someone opening up and operating a quarry of brownstone on the mainland. Last fall Captain Pike commenced operations on a quarry south of the village, and with characteristic push has succeeded in developing it to the extent that all doubts as to the practicality of the enterprise have vanished like fog before the rising sun, and the only question now to be met is how to supply the already existing demand for this high quality material.

At the point where the Captain opened this quarry there was considerable rough and shattered rock to be removed before the solid stone could be reached, but for this he found a ready use at a fairly remunerative figure in the way of filling for the Omaha docks at Washburn, and all winter long he has furnished employment to a large crew of men engaged in this work.

Several weeks since they reached bed rock, a sample was taken out, examined by experts in various cities and pronounced first-class in every respect. Orders soon followed on the heels of these reports. A large steam drill was at once purchased, a derrick erected, and the work force increased and work is now being pushed as rapidly as possible.

At this writing Mr. Pike has orders from various parties. From Minneapolis parties who propose to use his stone for brownstone fronts to brick buildings; from St. Paul parties who propose to use it for the same purpose and for coming to various buildings are Mr. Drake, of the latter city named, who is erecting a block of four-story buildings. He will use it in connection with stone from his jasper quarry at Sioux Falls.

The jasper, which is susceptible of a very high polish, will be used in that condition in the brownstone and the rough product, which will undoubtedly result in making it one of the most attractive blocks in that city. Thus the first seasons of operations of a quarry on the mainland starts out most auspiciously. The present facilities for handling and shipping this product of our country, to say nothing of the increased facilities for reaching the outside world promised us by the completion of the two great railway lines now building to this city, are visionary in predicting that the day is not far off when the brownstone from the Bayfield quarries will be in far greater demand for building purposes than any other stone on the continent, and that not one, but many of these quarries will be opened, developed and profitably worked.

A Good Showing for the First Year

Bayfield County Press - February 23, 1889

The following letter from the *Bayfield Brown Stone Company* to the Honorable David T. Day, of the United States Geological Survey, Washington DC demonstrates growth, scope and financial magnitude of the brownstone industry in Bayfield County.

Bayfield, Wisconsin February 13, 1889

Dear Sir:

The output of the *Bayfield Brown Stone Company* for the year 1888 was 358 carloads, valued at $14,000 at the quarries, against sales of from $40,000 the preceding year.

Last year being the presidential campaign year the sales in this vicinity fell off largely, but at the same time, the production continued and the quarry owners were enabled to get out large quantities of stone to have on hand in readiness for the early spring trade, the wisdom of which, they are already seeing, as they are all receiving fine orders for stone. The production continued in the *Bayfield Brown Stone Companies* quarry for 1888 was about $50,000 in round numbers.

Smith & Babcock are on the shore between Bayfield in Ashland and their output was about the same as ours. *Hartley Brothers*, who operate a quarry near them, also produced about the same. The *Prentice Brown Stone Company* opened a quarry last season and probably disposed of half this amount, what are preparing for a large business this coming year.

In 1889, the *Bayfield Brown Stone Company* will double last year's output, and the other quarries are figuring to do business in about the same proportion. We ship stone to St. Paul, Minneapolis, Omaha, Kansas City, St. Louis, Chicago, Cincinnati and Cleveland, and expect in the near future to ship to New York.

The stone is principally used in public buildings; but on account of its fineness, beauty and their stability, it is coming into use largely in private residences. The quality is fine and the quantity inexhaustible.

The total production in this vicinity for 1888 was perhaps 25% more than that of the preceding year, with the smaller output, but no decrease in values.

I have the honor to be your most obedient servant.
R. D. Pike, manager
Bayfield Brown Stone Company

Brown Stone Quarry: Bass Island
BHA Pike Research Center Archive Collection

Ships Loading Brownstone at Bass Island

Bayfield County Press - May 31, 1890

While the ship in the preceding photo may not necessarily be named the *Starlight*, the *Press* talks of such loading at Basswood Island.

"The brig named *Starlight* is now at Basswood Island, loading with brownstone for the Milwaukee Courthouse. She will take 500 tons this trip. The work in the quarry will still go on. Several large contracts are already made with different parties in Chicago, and the quarry will be taxed to the utmost to supply the demand. This stone is better as the work progresses and large quantities are being taken out. Some 700 tons await shipment at present. The company contemplates erecting three large buildings this summer, which, added to the present number, will make some 14 in all. About 50 hands are now at work and more laborers are wanted." *Bayfield Press,* June 24, 1871

Summer recreational activities for the young people of the Chequamegon Bay in the 1890s were practiced in a pure and simple form of leisure and exercise- row boating. Renting a double-seated dual-oared plug with a short tour in mind from one of the vender outlets on Bayfield's Front Street was a commonly called upon form of calm weather lake amusement. On the seats of the sixteen to twenty foot skiffs many young ladies in courtship mode, in fine dresses, were lavished upon further with the splash of an oar by the love-bitten suitor; many a brook trout

was caught off the dangling rod and minnow from the shallows of the rocky shoreline; many a championship rowboat race was held on the Fourth of July in the spirit of Uncle Sam and many a patron just went a-island hopping. A *Press* scribe and friends depart on a day trip to Basswood Island in 1890 and report to the weekly column with a chock-a-block review of their sightings.

Four of us rowed over from Bayfield to Bass Island in the early morning. The sun shone through the gray haze, the air was warm and balmy and the lake looked smooth as glass. In the distance we see the black smoke of an approaching steamer, and as we neared Bass Island we could see a large sailing vessel anchored near the shore, which had escaped our notice on account of being just round the head of the island. We found the water near the shore very clear and deep. We selected a pretty bit of sandy beach for a landing place and after an hour's hard rowing on a warm morning, it was with a feeling of pleasure that we felt the bottom of our boat grate over the smooth sand. One or two pushes with the oar and our boat was well the beach, and we stepped, for the first time on Bass Island.

A sailing vessel, which was lying near our landing place and which we had concluded must be a phantom ship, proved to be a large freight boat. Her crew was loading a cargo of brownstone. They had all about finished, however, and if the wind was fair would sail that afternoon. A very fine quality of brownstone is taken from this quarry on the island. The owners were not working the quarry at the time but had a large amount of stone on hand ready for shipment. I had often wondered, when I had seen these large blocks of stone lying in front of unfinished buildings, how the great stones were handled. But now a part of the mystery was explained, and, like everything else, proved to be easy enough when you know how.

These blocks are piled one upon the other in a semicircle, near the center of which stands a large derrick, operated by single horsepower. Each of these stones I noticed, were numbered and those of corresponding size placed upon the other with small boards or blocks in between. In the opening, thus left, the large stones were placed in the wake of the stones as they were uplifted through the host closely together in huge blocks would swing slowly around and were gradually lowered into their place into the hold of the vessel. The chains and ropes clank and croak so heavily each time that I wondered if they ever broke. I asked the captain, he replied, "yes, sometimes, but not often". The weight of the blocks was from 5 to 7 tons. The vessel carried about 5000 tons. I was much interested in examining one of the largest blocks to find a large piece of a petrified tree, firmly embedded in its center. The formation of sandstone around the petrified wood was white. I was determined to have a piece of the wood and also the stone and after hard work and patient perseverance we succeeded in getting a large piece of both wood and stone. I have it now before me, tied up in the very handkerchief I carried that day. I've never opened it.

Chapter Four
Peninsula Farms, Crops & Lifestyles

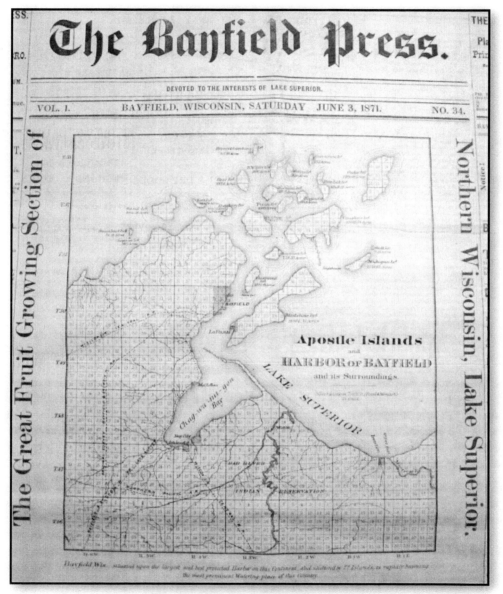

The Great Fruit Growing Section
BHA Pike Research Center Archive Collection

The Sunflower Patch at Sand Island
Anna, Johnny & Herman Johnson & Dorothy Hansen

BHA Pike Research Center Archive Collection
CON-D 2012.204.039

Apostle Islands & Mainland Farming

The map at the beginning the this chapter, of the government surveys will convey a better idea than any description we could give of the situation of the country about Bayfield, including the beautiful islands which form our harbor, and which, is completely shielded from storms. The map shows the size of each island in acres. The aggregate area is about fifty thousand acres. All the islands are heavily wooded; some of the larger having a great proportion of heavy pine and hemlock, while the others are bound with fine hardwood timber.

The soil is sandy loam, fertile, capable of producing fine crops and is especially adapted to fruit growing. This last statement will seem extravagant to some who are unacquainted with the surrounding conditions, but is entirely reasonable as the lake is materially modified by the vast surrounding body of deep water which, outside of Outer Island does not freeze in winter. By careful and accurate observations on an exposed portion of Michigan Island the past winter, it was found that ten degrees below zero was the coldest weather experience, while on the main shore but fifteen miles distant the mercury dipped to minus twenty-one degrees, a difference of eleven degrees in favor of the islands. *Bayfield Press* June 3, 1871

Farming and homesteading lifestyles in the Apostle Islands, Oak Island agriculture practices and a time capsule photo of Sand Island life and are previewed. Bayfield Ridge and mainland early agriculture follows. A chronological order of pioneer farm stories in the Apostle Island is followed by a visit to one of the early-on mainland farms at Hochdanner's farmhouse site, which also turns out to be possibly the earliest sportsman's lodge located upstream along the banks of Sioux River.

Lake Superior Farms

Bayfield County Press - **June 19, 1886**

In this almost primitive northern land, with its millions of tons of mineral wealth and its thousands of miles of pine forests, one might surmise that there was no room for agriculture, or perhaps no land suitable for cultivation. But that is not the fact. In many localities along the borders of the great Lake, and especially on various islands of the group known as the Apostles, the timber is mixed, hard and softwood, and of great variety. This, as is well-known, invariably produces a superior soil to all others. An intelligent vegetable farmer can realize from 10 acres of this land more substantial benefit then he could had from 100 acres of Dakota land.

The Apostle Islands offer unusually advantages to small farmers. You can build your homes from the timber on your land; you can work almost at home, for wages when not engaged on your own soil. You can raise enough potatoes on 2 acres the first year to pay for 160 acres of land. A home market is guaranteed for every variety of products. The great summer hotels in the vicinity will certainly require everything in the way of vegetables, poultry and dairy products that can be raised for years to come. The islands are by far the best place in the state for cultivation of fruits, especially of the smaller varieties. Nine different for right keys of wild berries grow here profusely. Stock raising would prove very profitable here as the winters are more temperate than on the mainland in the poorest land would produce 20 have tons of hay to the acre. Potatoes are a sure crop and are invariably of superior quality.

The soil on Madeline Island, the largest of the group, will average much better than any other locality of the same era in the lake region. It is somewhat more diversified than elsewhere, owing perhaps to its being deposited here in the remote past by great flood, or alteration of the Earth's surface. In places are to and even 3 feet of black mock, sufficient to enrich, if properly distributed, a dozen miles of barren sand. Then again, a large portion of the interior highlands are made up of a sandy loam resting above fine clay marl. At that time the American fur Company held fourth year, 1847, there were in bearing condition three fine orchards. Even to this day a remnant of an orchard in the shape of a cherry tree, also a few apple trees are to be seen."

Oak Island
Ashland County Plat Book - 1906

An Oak Island Farm &
the Mainland Farming Community

By Hank O. Fifield

Bayfield Press - October 27, 1870

Oak Island is being improved in the way of buildings quite rapidly. James Chapman & Company has put up one large dwelling and barn, besides several small buildings to be used by wood choppers through the winter.

The company designs getting several thousand cords of wood cut this winter for the purpose of supplying steamboats for next season. Last winter they put in a dock 400 feet long and we hear they propose enlarging it in the coming winter, so as to meet the increasing trade. It is their intention to clear the land as they go, and as fast as they divest it of wood, to plow and put in potatoes, grain, hay, etc. By this means they will soon have a large producing farm and not only get the benefit of the timber but of the soil also.

The soil of this island is said to be well adapted to agricultural purposes, have been well tested by Benjamin Armstrong, over ten years ago, whose house yet stands crumbling and wearing away by time and the elements. It would be greatly to the advantage of our businessmen, if they would devote more of their time and attention to farming. We hope at no distant day to see large fields of waving grain and grass, dotting the islands and mainland, presenting an ocular proof to visitors and people passing by of the fertility of the soil. (We have already satisfied ourselves on that score).

When this is done and not until then, will we have an influx of emigrants from the farming community; then we will hear the ring of the axe and crashing of fallen trees from daylight to darkness of night, and in an incredible short time the soil occupied exclusively by timber, will be large fields of all kinds of vegetables and grains adapted to this climate, which will enliven and build up business and trades of every description. Then the boats of this lake will not have to go back on their down trips empty as they do now, but would be filled with the produce of our farmers.

The farming class of our emigrants as a general thing are men of limited means and are not easily tempted by fine speeches to invest the "little all" until they see conclusively that the land will produce as presented; and this is why that men owning land and doing business here should devote part of the attention to farming, for it is nothing more than a proof of the value of these lands.

When we get a farming community around us our land will be more valuable, the mercantile business will increase and in fact, all branches of trade will began to flourish. And it is the remark of all new comers, "why do you not devote more attention to farming, your soil is good; we see no reasons for not putting your advantages to practical use"? The only excuse that can be offered for this neglected branch of industry is that nearly all of our business men are engaged in the wood, lumber and fish trade, and have neglected the improving of the land almost entirely. But people owning land here, are beginning to open their eyes to the vast amount of wealth laying latent in the soil.

What little effort has been made this, proved, most satisfactory as the samples at Chapman & Co.'s store will, collected by J. D. Cruttendon, Esquire from the gardens of different people of this town—consisting of some of the finest specimens of potatoes, beets, turnips and squash that ever graced the tables of county fairs in any state.

Some of the finest oats we ever saw were raised by John Buffalo, Indian Chief of the Red Cliff Band, in Buffalo Bay, and we believe that if our citizens should give it a fair trial the result would prove most gratifying to all. Spring wheat has been successfully raised here, and will eventually become one of the leading staples our farmers. Hay that can be raised in abundance and 2 ½ to 3 tons per acres is considered but a medium crop and always commands from 20-25 dollars per ton. Yet with these tempting prospects laying out before our citizens, but little has been done in the way of farming; and they have preferred to turn their attention in other directions, but we are glad to see the farming interest improving and believe that our citizens will finally take hold of it with a will—We would also state that apples can and are being raised, both in Bayfield and La Pointe.

The soil of this section has many advantages which other places on the lake do not possess. Here it is of a light sandy loam which retains the heat of the sun, causing vegetation to put forth earlier and mature sooner, than were it of that cold, stiff and sticky clay which you find further up the lake. And upon a whole, when the farming interest is once fairly started in this section it will equal any in the state.

Sand Island Farm Life

Circa Early 1900s

Family of Elvis and Marguerite Moe Collection

The photo above presents Louis Moe, with a watchful eye on a calf on Sand Island pasture land while a youthful Fred Hansen, 5th right, ponders the jointly held conversation. The practice to farm, lumber, along with operating an established fish camp on the island started in the mid-1880s with Frank Shaw at Shaw Point. Here he and wife Josephine Dutcher-Shaw located on the southeast sandpoint, about one mile from the mainland's Little Sand Bay, and raised a large family year around on the island. Commercial fishing via pound nets was Shaw's principle income source. For the root cellar and as a cash crop the family started a small orchard and raised a large garden with surplus strawberries, raspberries, potatoes, any vegetable not used fresh or in the canning process was sent to Bayfield and mainland markets on their private vessels. Frank Shaw's son-in-law Solly Boutin's *Herring King* tug, or the A. Booth & Sons fishery pick-up boats like the *S.B. Barker, T.H. Camp, Helen* and *C.W. Turner* also freighted additional produce.

Peter and Constance Hansen, an elder Fred and Agnetta Hansen along with the Bert and Birgit Noreng family, the Herman and Hattie Johnson Sr. and Louis and Nana Moe families located their homesteads and fish docks north of Shaw Point at East Bay, near to Justice Bay and Sand Island Lighthouse. At this East Bay homestead location many a Sand Islander family raised their children, sent the offspring to the Sand Island School, mended their nets and fished gill nets through the ice from January through April. Playing cards with neighbors on the cold and windswept winter nights, dances, or reading the weekly news of America's Doughboy soldiers fighting WWI & II antagonists in France and worldwide campaigns served as activity fillers. Sorry to report, this unspoiled lifestyle ended when the year-around residents departed the island forever in 1944.

Farming Amongst the Apostle Islands

Dated Excerpts from the *Bayfield Press*

The following chronological documentation represents a time period prior to Oak and Sand Island cultures and introduces the origin of the practice of orcharding on the Apostle Islands which application later lead to present day industrial orchards in the Bayfield Peninsula that were established circa 1906. Note that the information presented hereafter is recognized in the time period from 1870 - 1882 and gleaned from Hank O. Fifield's *Bayfield Press*.

October 27, 1870: Mr. Pendergast of Michigan Island Light, who is an old nurseryman, informs us that he is confident apple trees can be to bear thriftly here, and he has started a nursery on that island of several thousand trees, and intends to give it a thorough trial. It is a mistaken idea that we are too far north to follow agricultural pursuits. With a good soil, no frosts until late in October, our winters no longer and not as cold as those 160 miles south of us, we can safely count this one of the finest farming localities in the state.

Further evidence of the Apostle Islands as growing zone: Editor- Press—- Oak Island is being improved in the way of buildings quite rapidly. James Chapman & Company has put up one large dwelling and barn, besides several small buildings to be used by wood choppers through the winter. The company designs upon getting several thousand cords of wood cut this winter for the purpose of supplying steamboats for next season.

Last winter Chapman and William Knight put in a dock 400 feet long and we hear they propose enlarging it in the coming winter, so as to meet the increasing trade. It is their intention to clear the land as they go, and as fast as they divest it of wood to plow and put in potatoes, grain, hay, etc. By this means they will soon have a large producing farm and not only get the benefit of the timber but of the soil also.

February 4, 1871: As soon as the ice is sufficiently strong to admit it, Chapman and Company, will add several cribs to their dock at Oak Island. A dance occurred at Oak Island on Monday evening, in which the elite to that place participated.

October 26, 1871: Steamboat men will do well to procure their wood at Oak Island as it is on the regular steamboat channel with good dockage facilities, the water being twenty feet and upward at the landing. Chapman and Company have a large quantity of dry wood for sale at reasonable rates. Steamboat men will please bear these facts in mind."

May 13, 1871: We learn that Henry M. Rice has a man at work on his island, clearing land, preparatory to farming. He proposes to try fruit growing also. Success to that enterprise!

On June 1, 1868, the United States of America, by President Andrew Johnson, under the Seal of the U. S. General Land Office affixed to Henry M. Rice an island, so named Rice's island earliest on, and is now identified as Rocky Island. The property transfer was first recorded on September 19, 1867. The kind of instrument used was a U. S. Patent with a date of record registered as January 7, 1880. Remarks offered stated, "Given under an Act of Congress, approved July 12, 1862, entitled, an Act Donating Public Lands to the several States and Territory, which may provide for Colleges for the benefit of Agriculture and the Mechanical Arts."

May 20, 1871: The schooner *Alice Craig* left this port on Thursday for Michigan Island with an assorted cargo. Her manifest consisted of several yoke of cattle, farming implements, and seed, for Mr. Pendergast, who proposes to till the soil and reap a rich harvest of the necessities of life, as well as raising apples, etc., in his promising nursery. In a very few years the islands hereabouts will contain many rich producing farms as well as thrifty orchards.

June 3, 1871: A nursery planted on Michigan Island has endured two winters triumphantly, and young trees are very hardy and vigorous. All the fruit trees on the main shore are thriving. We recently saw some exceedingly large and thrifty trees, loaded with blossoms, on one of the islands. Ex-Senator Stearns of Minnesota, an experienced horticulturist, has lately visited the islands and made thorough investigations of their adaptability to fruit growing; the results of which are that he has purchased 640 acres of land on one of these islands and, in connection with capitalists whom he represents, proposes to enter extensively on the cultivation of fruit."

June 3, 1871: On the South end of Ironwood Island, are the remains of several buildings erected many years since by the American Fur Company. One, probably was used as a warehouse, was some 70 feet in length by 20 in width, indicating a large business at that point. The island was not occupied for some 35 years. This spring the owner of the island who, with his family, has removed to the island a month since. Already several acres are cleared and a portion planted with potatoes. The soil is a dark loam and the fine growth of timber indicates great strength and fertility.

July 8, 1871: The apples on the islands look well. Martin Rheum has several fine fruit trees at Ashland that promise well.

August 9, 1871: In strolling about town a day or two since we notice in the garden of John McDonald, Esquire, six or seven trees loaded down with fine large apples. They're different kinds and the thrifty fruit are promising well. One small tree looked about 6 feet high and as hearty looking a fruit as we ever saw, most of which were as large as coffee cups and just turning red being a fall apple.

Several trees bear winter apples and are a good size. That this section is good for fruit raising there is not the least doubt, said agricultural Editor Ford of the St. Paul Press. He visited here not long since and in his examination of fruit trees secured several small, insignificant apples from a neglected apple tree on Madeline Island and pronounced them as being fair specimens of Lake Superior fruit. If you have seen the apples in McDonald's yard he was somewhat different to as regards this section been a fruit growing region. Above the village of LaPointe, about 2 miles, an old Frenchman has a number of trees bearing heavily this year; apples being of large size and finest qualities. Cherries raised successfully in large quantities are secured from the islands and the main shore.

September 2, 1871: Mr. Pendergast of Michigan lighthouse showed us some oats a day or two since, that were raised by him on Michigan Island. They are as fine a looking oats as one would wish to see, and he claims that his field will average with the specimen. He says that his apple trees look splendid and those trees that bear are thrifty, the fruit being hardy and of the choicest kind.

From an excerpt from Editor Leonard, of the *Red Wing, Minnesota Argus*; "through one of the outer channels in the blue distance eastward, was pointed out Michigan Island, and where on an enterprising horticulturist has established a nursery of fruit trees and shrubbery, and has, in their second season of healthy growth, young apple trees."

September 16, 1871: The cranberry crop promises a splendid yield in this section, and already large amounts have been picked by the Indians. They bring a fair price and find a ready market.

Pendergast of Michigan Island raised 60 bushel of oats to the acre at that place this season. His fruit trees are looking well.

September 23, 1871: Pendergast of Michigan Island presented us as a finest specimen of the "Early Rose" potato as we ever saw. They were planted on June 15 and the largest one weighed nearly three pounds. His corn and beans look splendid. He showed us a bouquet of pansies – that was large, beautiful and fragrant.

In a separate article in this edition, noted is; " In the company with Judge R. R. Nelson, Franklin Steele and some other old time Minnesotans, we took a boat at Bayfield to LaPointe, where we found the apple and cherry trees raised some 30 odd years ago by the father of Mr. Oakes of St. Paul. This is an orchard in an old settlement, and everything has a truly ancient appearance.

The apple trees also showed signs of decay either from age or the hard winters. The fruit of these pioneers is not very large, and they seem to be rather inferior seedlings. At Bayfield we thought some trees also showed signs of pretty cold weather. Now this is just the point to get at in the discussion of the fruit question. It will not be safe to make calculations for the future on what we really saw at either Bayfield or LaPointe. The choice grafted sorts of apples may not be as well as the "Oakes Seedlings." The cherries are the common Morello or pie cherries of the East. In fact, the trial has not been general enough to warrant any correct opinion on the subject. Mr. Pendergast's experience of one of the islands will be more satisfactory.

At La Pointe it is no better for fruit than on the land, as it is not far enough in the lake to be benefited by the water. The soil, however, where the old trees are growing, is stiff red clay, while at Bayfield sand predominates. This of course, is decidedly in the favor of the pioneer orchard. We shall look before the experiment done at Michigan Island with no little interest, as there are many kinds planted, and are cared for by an experienced fruit grower. On Michigan Island, Mr. Pendergast, formerly of Minneapolis, has commenced quite an extensive orchard; a growing number of years will be required to demonstrate to the outside world that he will be really successful.

During my visit at Bayfield I chanced to meet Mr. Pendergast, from whom I learned many important facts in connection with this new enterprise. If we remember his statement in regard to the extreme of cold in winter, it was not so much as at Bayfield by at least 10°. Residents at Bayfield told us that the thermometer did not indicate nearly so great a degree of cold as at St. Paul, while about the lake they are not so dry in winter; this is very important in the consideration of fruit culture. Another is that in spring there is not as much danger from late frosts, as well as early freezing in autumn. The islands, of course, are more favorably located in this respect than the mainland. (From Agricultural Editor Ford, St. Paul Press; *Fruit Capacity of the Lake Region*)

October 3, 1877: The *Ashland Press* proposes to agriculturists in Ashland and Bayfield Counties, to place on exhibition specimens of their productions at the post office, and the charge of James A. Wilson, Esquire, who has kindly consented to furnish a suitable place to show the productions, and to arrange them properly for exhibition. This is a good suggestion, and we hope all farmers in Bayfield County will at once, during this beautiful weather, send in their average specimens of their crops, properly directed. The *Eva Wadsworth* will no doubt transport the articles at a very small price, and probably free of charge.

Farmer McCloud, Bass Island, should send down some samples, for he has devoted a number of years to raising fine vegetables, and has given considerable study two varieties.

Mr. Wilson is a most competent man. He is one of the largest producers in this section, and has given a good deal of study to agriculture and horticulture, as well as having been a close observer in these matters.

Let a good show be made, and be done without delay. Let farmers Pike, Stark, McElroy, Hochdanner, Roth, Hoefle, Atkinson and all the rest be heard from. All articles sent should be so marked that Mr. Wilson will know who sent them, and the lands upon which they were raised, with such other items of information as well give interest to the exhibition. *Ashland Daily Press*

October 17, 1877: William Herbert Sr., was in from his farm on Ironwood Island last week with a fine lot of vegetables, among which was a big tomato, which weighed 2 pounds, 2 ounces.

November 28, 1877: Last Wednesday, the famous farmer of Bass Island, West McCloud, dropped into the *Press* office and left in our charge numerous samples of his work from the island. Among them were four or five mammoth onions of the red and white flat variety, some of them measuring 5 inches in diameter, and three inches from top to bottom; some splendid field corn, each year measuring a foot in length, and sometimes more, and well filled with beautiful, amber like grains.

The wheat, however, was what claimed our principal attention. It has always been claimed that winter wheat could not be raised in this country, unless protected by a good, thick blanket of snow. The wheat in question was raised on an open, unprotected piece of ground, which the wind kept clear of snow all winter. Still the wheat will compare favorably with the average Minnesota or Illinois grain. The articles may be seen on exhibition in the *Press* office window, that is, all that's left of them, some of our visitors have borrowed some the finest when our back was turned.

January 23, 1878: A serious and painful accident befell Mr. William Herbert, Sr. last Friday. While chopping wood on at his farm on Ironwood Island, a tree he was at work at fell a little sooner than he expected it to, striking him in the lower portion of the left leg, breaking it near the ankle. His two boys, Charlie and Jimmy, managed to get him to the house, and then drag a heavy boat from way up on the beach to the water, a feat that would have been hard work for two able-bodied men, and went over to Mr. Herbert's aid, providing aid and they soon had him into town.

September 18, 1878: West McCloud, of Bass Island, is truly the boss agriculturists of this region. He has placed on exhibition in the *Press* office, a monstrous tomato, weighing exactly 2 pounds. He also brought in from the island, some fine musk and watermelons, which in size and flavor fully equal those of the sunny South.

October 9, 1878: West McCloud has placed on exhibition in Fred Fisher's saloon a squash that weighs 60 pounds. It is another one of the Basswood Island products. Tuesday, October 8, West placed on our table some splendid specimens of the Ives, Hartford, and Concord varieties of grapes which are grown on his Bass Island farm.

October 23, 1878: West McCloud, the champion farmer of Bass Island, has sold his farm to Robert Pew of Buffalo Bay, and left for St. Paul. Mr. McCloud's place was the first ever taken under the Homestead Act, {an act passed by the U.S. Congress in 1862, promising ownership of 160 acres of public land to a citizen who lived on and cultivated it for five years} in the Bayfield District. We are sorry that the genial and open-handed West sees fit to leave us.

A Sportsman's Paradise at Sioux River

By Guest Contributor- John A. Butler

Bayfield County Press - October 3, 1885

On October 24, 1885, the *Bayfield County Press* notes: "[The] Henry Hochdanner family at their Sioux River farm as having put up something over 65 tons of tame hay". Not only was the Hochdanner family an early pioneer farming family which raised a cornucopia's worth full of field plants and timothy hay, but they also took advantage of tourists and voyagers venturing to Bayfield on the recently opened Chicago, St. Paul, Minneapolis & Omaha Railway to Bayfield. Here Mr. John A. Butler, position or rank unknown, of St. Louis, Missouri writes to the column and remarks about Henry Hochdanner's farm on the Sioux River and of his delightful experience fishing the "big rock" waters of this Chequamegon Bay tributary.

Without any intention of competing with the original discoveries of Lake Superior, the region about it had a few years ago so fallen out of notice that it became, in a humble way, my privilege to discover it again. I learned, however, that in the course of many pleasant northern trips, there has been one important spot to which I have never once referred, and that is "Hochdanner's" on the Sioux River. The reader may never have heard of this place before, and I believe, with peculiar independence, that it has never aspired to be noticed in a literary way, the fame being a matter of report among its many patterns. "Hochdanner's", in fact, aspires to nothing. It is sufficient to itself, and simply demands in a pleasantly imperative way the respectful deference of traveling writers, and the appreciative recognition of the general public.

There is nothing negative or cringing about Hochdanner's, and in the same breath in which I became aware of my neglected duty as an aspiring member of the press, I also learned that "if you don't gif de pipple some trout on the table, Mr. Butler, dat can't go fishing derselves, you haf to pay next year more, Mr. Butler and no mistake, ain't it!" (Mrs. Henry Hochdanner)

A delightful English gentleman, Doctor H. of Madison and his wife, who are connected with all the pleasant things of this country and England in a literary and social way, both in the present and in the past, called my attention one day to a motto in "Hochdanner's" parlor. It was not one of those mawkish and ostentatious prayers, in red letters, but at the very least an original selection, although the sentiment is old. In the corner near the stove, a little out-of-the-way, with a suggestion of reserve, were the words; "Labor Has a Sure Reward." It seemed to come from the personality of a certain thrifty, kindhearted older housewife, and is at the foundation of everything at Sioux River. The very persistence and earnestness of character there is one of the things that compels the present writing, in the long and strange sequence of human events, and in spite of all I ever paid to Mister and Misses Hochdanner in money. I am no doubt still her debtor, in some inexplicable way, for ever having visited her at all; and it was undoubtedly the same potential for signage that inscrutably called General Bragg and other devoted trout fisherman to a yearly pilgrimage to the valley of the Sioux River.

The reader by this time wonders where and what "Hochdanner's" may be. Let me say in a word that it consists of a grassy valley in the heart of the wilderness; dark whispering pines on the surrounding hills, with their lofty tops forever waving back and forth against the sky. At the head of the valley a winding stream issues from the cool and rocky gorges of the hills and goes laughing and dancing to the sunny valley down to the blue waters of Lake Superior. For the rest there are flocks of croaking crows, with glossy plumage glistening in the sun; a picturesque whitewashed log cabin, surrounded by flowers, with a high peaked roof and a sweet water well; snug log stables; cattle with tinkling bells; lank, baying hounds, whose voices echo amid the hills, and a fleecing morning mist that arises in clouds, on summer days, in an atmosphere clearer than the purest crystal. This is the Sioux River Valley, but although there are others residing there, I am convinced that it would all go for nothing if it were not for the wrinkled, indefatigable, voluble little old German woman, whose heart is in her mild, patient, old husband, and in the future of two sons, who are a sort of compromise between the sons of the old German forest and the lumbermen and hunters of the North, but who will no doubt tone down to the manners and wisdom of the traditional host in time to come.

In Mrs. Hochdanner, on the contrary, those venerable characteristics were largely embodied at her birth, along with some emphasis of the worldly prudence peculiar to her race. With her are to be associated an abundance of blueberries, saucers flowing with cream, tender venison roasts, waffles, flaky potatoes, a clean orderly house, trout done to a turn, your meals when you want them, and from one dollar twenty to one dollar fifty cents a day. The reader has my conception of the hostess of Sioux River, but before I left she became so important a personage, that Sioux River in the beautiful valley through which it flows, seems to have transferred to a mere appendage.

The Sioux River: I do not know that the Sioux River can be found on any applet code unless it be a map of Bayfield County or the charts of the Wisconsin Central Railway. Through Ms. Hochdanner it has acquired an original location which cannot be stated in ordinary terms. It lies beyond the railways and outside of the modern world. It lies in the heart of the land and rests in a quite unique environment of woods and streams and was no doubt made by Ms. Hochdanner herself after some modest model in the lower Bavarian Alps.

The Hochdanner's cannot tell you anything about it at the Colby House in Ashland, and seem never to have heard of this existence. At the Chequamegon Hotel they know where it lies, and that establishment in its quietness is one of the nearest artificial approaches to it I have ever seen, but I presume there are many close by who do not know of its existence and to whom "Hochdanner" is not a meaningful term. After dwelling so long on talk doubters and Sioux River it would be impertinent to speak at length of my own experience there. I was tired. The last days of the trouting season were at hand. I wanted to spend more time where I knew I would certainly be successful. I did not care for the abundance of more remote and wholly unfair streams. I prefer to come stealthily upon my prey, to wander far up cool, rocky valleys, casting the flies at the foot of the foaming rapids from a cautious distance, dropping them noiselessly along the deep pools, and in shadowy, covert nooks, and catching perhaps the only trout there, grown old, and large, and wary, in his long avoidance to artificial lures.

I noticed the stream that has been fished for fifteen years, many visitors of this season, fishing casually, have left a record in the register of six hundred to one thousand trout apiece, many of them weighing between one and three pounds. My own modest efforts of a few days in waters disturbed by heavy rains and bursting lumber dams yielded all I wanted to eat and two hundred trout for friends at home. Besides this, I shot at several deer with a revolver, helped to bring home a bear, and had a visit from one of those dark and heavy sons of the forest one day as I ate my dinner on the rocks in the middle the stream. I also had the experience of seeing a beautiful fawn come bounding down the rapids at my feet, to remain like a vision of beauty for a moment, and then dart away with incredible ease and speed through a tangle of underbrush that seems to preclude escape.

The Woods and Streams: Quite near, in the vicinity of Ashland and Bayfield, the woods still swarm with game. As long as Lake Superior remains a cold reservoir that it is, innumerable trout will always replenish the streams in the fall in spite of the most diligent fishing, unless they continue to be slaughtered in the winter with dynamite at the headwaters. If people would refuse to buy trout after September, which begins the wholesome spawning season, the fish might be had indefinitely in the season when they are most delicious; and the wholesome and invigorating sport of trout fishing would become what it still remains in England and other portions of the old world where a restraining wisdom is exercised with success.

I regret to lift the veil exposing Sioux River and Hochdanner's to the world. It seems like invading the privacy of nature to which only the simple life of simple people is as can, I hope only those worthy of this life will go there. Happily the pines and crows, the log cabin and the sweet well, will remain for some time to come; the river will tumble musically through its rocky riffles and sunny shadows, and comes singing and sparkling and hurdling through the meadows.

I do not wish to contemplate the time when a busy, bustling hotel, with an inscrutable nonchalant clerk, with carefully brushed hair, shall invade the Valley of the Sioux River. I am very much afraid that Mrs. Hochdanner in her inner consciousness contemplates some approximation to those horrible ideas. That, however, is only to come when she is dead and certainly shall not, while she is still alive. I am forced, however, to say that she has, in addition to her picturesque log cabin, a large wooden building, painted in the prevailing colors, with a red roof, which is said to be a very comfortable abode. I suppose it is for those who hope someday to see the buses and railroad car in the Sioux River Valley. For myself, with those who wear blue flannel shirts or blue seaside dresses, and like a quiet, contemplative life, plain, homey fare, pleasant sport, and escape from the thralldom of stiff lawns, the modern house and its belongings, and all the unpoetic life of fashion and convention, I prefer in the old log cabin.

A short sojourn only too soon found out the inevitable. One day I rode with Herr Hochdanner slowly through the clear air and down through the silent woods to the dark bluish Chequamegon Bay, which looked rare and lustrous, and full of strange, pulsing, regal life of its own. The Apostle Islands lay against the eastern horizon, like huge, sleeping leviathans, with their huge regular, oval backs above the water. The sun was sinking fast, and the waters of the bay rapidly changed to a delicate shell pink. In the middle distance there were broad reaches of soft waves, grayish green and purple, with a soft blue band along the horizon in the outer lake.

The lighthouse at Chewamic Point and fishing shanties gleamed warmly in the sun, on the distant islands. Finally, by some subtle art of nature, the growths along the beach seemed on the actual horizon. The gray of the broad vision being beyond became atmospheric and transparent. Blue horizon lay beneath a dull, purplish haze, like a low-flying winter cloud, and the day had reached its end.

Then came the scream of the locomotive, the newspapers, English politics, the plague, civil service, and the latest scandal of the day, and I was once more in the busy, bustling world.

William Knight tending his Apple Orchard Circa 1910
Location: T. 50 N.-R.4-3-W Sections 10 & 11 on County Highway J.

Scott Knighten Hale & BHA Pike Research Center Archive Collection

Establishment of the Bayfield Peninsula Fruit Industry

By Editor- C. E. Patterson

Bayfield Progress - September 24, 1914

"Where these trees grow and were harvested only once, why not plant trees that will yield a harvest every year?" said William Knight, first chairman of the Bayfield Horticultural Society and foremost Bayfield orchardist at the outset of the industrial orchard and fruit growing era circa 1906. Eleanor Knight in her book, *Tales of Bayfield Pioneers*, and whose grandfather William Knight is the bearer of the idea, goes on to say that he "assembled men, horses and dynamite and began to work on the stumps. As fast as the land was cleared he planted fruit trees. This was all an experiment, because up to this time no one thought fruit could be raised commercially year."

Good it is that William Knight studied first the results of 1870s orcharding work of Roswell Pendergast on Michigan Island and closely watched the back yard apple growers in town harvest their private crops year after year. From those conclusions and amongst conversation with South Dakota apple cultivator and propagator Charles H. Whiting [1] along with Harvey Nourse at the society meetings planted his first trees in 1906; 20 acres in cherries and 20 acres in apples. On May 18, 1906 the *Bayfield County Press* offers, "William Knight is setting out 2000 fruit trees this week. Mr. Knight has the land, the means and the disposition to make an orchard and he's going to do it."

Editor C. E. Patterson updates the reader to genesis the peninsular fruit industry history. The apple industry and orchards, located just a mile just over the big hill, from the Harbor City, to this day remains an active and viable industry. Here begins the review:

William Knight, Frank Holston, Orlando Flanders, Curtis T. Andreas of Bayfield, Charles Whiting of Yankton, South Dakota and Dan Maxy of Washburn are the dreamers who built the fruit and apple industry for Bayfield County read the subtitle on this date.

Surely it took some imagination a dozen years ago to seriously urge fruit production in the farthest north section of Wisconsin. Values were measured in board feet in those days, just as a generation before, values were measured in furs and sometimes fish. The history of the old trading of Bayfield is a series of events involving Indians, French traders, John Jacob Astor, furs and lumber. Astor had a presence in his time not possessed by any other living man. He argued that at the western end of Lake Superior would grow a great city. He proceeded to say that at the southern end of Lake Michigan would grow up another great city and while he argued, he was doing a tidy business in the vicinity of Bayfield and the little trading post across the channel on Madeline Island.

Cherries were growing on Madeline Island in Astor's time. The Chippewa Indians related that the trees were planted by the French explorers. The cherries grew abundantly and in turn other trees were planted and grafted from the original stock. Indians eighty years old will say the cherries were there even when they were children. The furs are gone and Astor is gone. The timber has gone and the Indians are few, but the cherries are still growing. These cherries were the inspiration to the men, who but a dozen years ago were laughed at for their dreams. "Nature is kind to the shore acres; why not develop the fruit industry?" If cherries will grow and stand the tests of cold and frosts- why not apples?" Now the few harmless lunatics of a decade ago are living to see their prophecies come true. They are the wise men of the peninsula and have one on John Jacob Astor, who did not live to see the fulfillment of his long distance forecasts.

Ten thousand bushels of apples will be shipped out of Bayfield this year. The first car load was billed on the September 11th 1914. It will take twenty cars to accompany the crop. The orchards of fifty growers are this year yielding the first commercial crops. In the Washburn District, eighteen orchards will ship their products. William Knight of Bayfield will ship a crop estimated at four thousand bushels, and Ed Stevens of Washburn will ship four hundred bushels from his four year old orchard. From the orchards now planted, the shipment in the year 1919 is estimated as five hundred cars from Bayfield alone. Since 1910, strawberries, currants, cherries and blackberries have been car lot commodities from Bayfield, but apples are just coming into commercial consideration.

Some peach trees are approaching the time when they too will add to the volume of shipments from Bayfield and Washburn

The oldest commercial orchard in Bayfield is eight years old. It was planted by William Knight who has been something of a father to the industry since its inception. August Turnquist, a farmer began to turn public opinion his way about twelve years ago, when he planted a small orchard. Of course the light keepers on the islands set out trees sixty and seventy years ago, and one Roswell Pendergast set out a considerable amount of trees on Michigan Island about forty years ago according to Dad Davis, proprietor of the Bayfield's Davis Hotel.

The history of fruit growing is very recent. It involves the operations of real estate men, with a financial interest in the success of the enterprise. Be it said to their credit, that unlike their ilk in western lands, they saw the wisdom of slow growth and saw the evils of over exploitation. The Bayfield peninsula fruit industry so far has not suffered the reaction of a boom. Markets and cheap transportation located near have saved the industry from the common disaster of the more advertised sections. In the beginning, the advocates of orcharding wisely decided that no permanent industry could be built unless effort was concentrated on a very small area for experimental purposes. On this theory was established the "red line", an arbitrary line drawn on the map to establish a "frost proof district." How many miles south of the shore line of Lake Superior one can successfully grow tree fruits on a commercial scale, no one is prepared to stake his reputation, but the "red line" has steadily moved south to meet the exigencies of real estate deals and now includes Washburn. The humorous fiction of the "red line" has really been a blessing, because it has built up a community of fruit growers and has concentrated the interests, much to the market advantage of all concerned.

Then too, the community plan has made for sanity in the planting of tried varieties. [2] It has eliminated the pests and unscrupulous tree agents. Scarcely any of the growers were in the beginning trained orchard men. They have had to learn by experience and from each other. The dreamers of a dozen years ago took to the State Fair in Milwaukee at that time about three apples on a plate. They lied like gentlemen and waxed eloquent over prospects. None believed them and they stood for much spoofing and humor. Now the only regret of the forecasters in that they did not romance more. They could have lied more and still have told the truth.

[1] 11, November, 1905: George H. Whiting, the widely known nurseryman of Yankton, S. D. purchased 1000 acres of Carver, Qsuayle, & Nourse. The land is located four miles southwest of Bayfield on the shores of Lake Superior, through which the Omaha runs ten daily trains. This 1,000 acre farm is to be cleared up and devoted solely to growing fruit. It is Mr. Whiting's boast that in five years he will load the biggest lake vessel from his own docks with apples and other fruits from this orchard. [Author's note: This property extends from the Whiting Road and is located on the hillside near east of Van Tassel's Point]

[2] "Duchess" of Oldenburg, Wealthy, Dudley, Yellow Transparent, Patten Greening, Northwestern Greening, Whitney Crab apple, and Transcendental Crab apple were early cultivars.

Harvey Nourse Sr. Farm & Strawberry Patch
Salmo Station: Circa 1910
BHA Pike Research Center Archive Collection

From obituary content noted it was that Harvey Nourse Sr. was born in Bayfield, February 20th 1870 and died in 1949. Nourse was one of eleven children born to early Presbyterian missionary Joseph Harvey and Isabelle Rittenhouse-Nourse. At the time of his death he was reputed to be the longest-time native-born resident in the Chequamegon region. Mr. Nourse lived his later years at Salmo station, a cluster of residencies three miles south of Bayfield at which the Omaha Railway stopped. Nourse was a prominent pioneer farmer and a standing member and leader of the Bayfield Horticultural Society in which he often attended the Wisconsin State Fair and lectured in the New Wisconsin about horticultural practices. On his property overlooking the thirteen acre berry patch and Lake Superior was a prime woodland maple grove stand which harbored the family sugar maple processing camp.

Harvey was one of 11 children born to his missionary father Joseph and mother Isabelle Rittenhouse-Nourse. The father was first located in Pennsylvania, and was then sent to the Indian Territory in Oklahoma. Here his health failed and he was sent to Bayfield in 1856 to rest, not being expected to live. Joseph H. Nourse was one of Bayfield's first white settlers. He recovered his health and lived at Bayfield many years, starting the Presbyterian Church there and acted as one of the first school teachers at Bayfield.

In his younger days the son Harvey was a missionary singer, and for a time sang in the lumber camps of north Wisconsin at evangelistic meetings at which the late Reverend Alfred

Terry, father of the head of the lakes singer Elizabeth Terry, was the preacher. A year ago Mr. Nourse, although 78, sang a duet with Miss Terry at her Bayfield sacred concert, and then sang a solo, "Tell Me the Old, Old Story."

Harvey Nourse Strawberries

Iron River Pioneer & Bayfield Progress July 6, 1911

Headed by "Brother P. J. Savage, the able editor and municipal judge of the Iron River Pioneer Press, a representative party came over to Bayfield with to view the orchards, Bayfield's big berries and fields lead off this descriptor of life in close proximity to the banks of the Pike's Creek.

Leaving Bayfield early in the morning by auto and livery the party drove in a south and westerly direction, visiting the farms of Frank V. Holston, Harvey Nourse, Morris Ryder, Henry Sykes and the "state experimental farm" at Salmo. On every field the berry pickers, for the most part girls and young ladies, were as busy as bees and carrying them to the temporary sorting and checking houses which are found on every field. Two systems of picking are in vogue. Some have men employed in carrying the berries from the field to the central station, while others require the pickers to deliver their berries themselves.

A tag is issued to each picker every morning with their number thereon corresponding with the number the picker has in a record which is kept by the manager of the plantation. As the pickers deliver a tray of four quarts at the station or to the carrier, as the case may be, the tag is punched, with a punch procured for that purpose. In the evening the tags are turned in, and each one credited with the number of quarts indicated on the tag. This system has been found to be the simplest and most reliable of any tried and is generally most adopted by the growers.

The largest field we visited were owned or leased by Harvey Nourse. He had thirteen acres in fruit this year, and to harvest this crop he required the services of sixty-eight pickers. Of the sixty-eight, but three were boys and we found that they were, for the most part from Superior—-girls who are students in the schools in that city. Two or three teachers from Superior were also there, and they acted as chaperons for the girls and at the same time performed some work in connections with checking and sorting.

On the Nourse farm we found that a building had been constructed to accommodate the pickers and to meet the requirements of the berry farm. It was a two story affair, possibly 30 x 60 feet, and two stories in height. The first floor was divided by a partition extending the whole length of the building. On one side was a spacious dining hall and kitchen in the rear, and the other was a storehouse for berry boxes and other little devices as used in putting crates together. The second story consisted of a large ward, well ventilated and screened, where the pickers slept.

The plants at the Nourse farm were set out last year and the stand there was very fine and the plants well loaded with fruit in various stages of development from small green berries to large, ripe ones. The soil there was a mixture of clay and sand, with a larger percentage of clay than sand. It was at the base of a large hill where the seepage kept the ground moist most of the time and tended to supply the much needed moisture for an abundant crop. While much depends upon the weather conditions of the next ten days, yet this field will undoubtedly produce not less than 500 crates to the acre. The two year old fields and those not heavily mulched which were one year old, seemed to be further advanced and did not produce such luxuriant foliage, nor as many nor as large berries, the variety considered.

At twenty-one years of age Harvey Nourse was a practicing farmer at a site near where the Onion River flows into Lake Superior. In the *Washburn News* printed in the *Bayfield County Press* on November 9, 1901 the press man visits Mr. Nourse at his 240 acre farm site located near the banks of the Onion River. Here is the report of this day trip.

This property is now in the high state of cultivation. Mr. Nourse has clearly demonstrated by the present condition of his farm that he is one of the most progressive agriculturists in the state and those who knew the property before he became proprietor are probably aware of what he had to contend with in order to bring it to its present excellent condition; for two seasons he lost his crop by the overflow the river. In order to obviate that, he changed the stream, which entailed a large amount of arduous labor and expense and is satisfactory to know he is now reaping the benefits of his enterprise.

The past season has been a prosperous one as a detail of the products will show. There was shipped from the farm 500, 16 quart cases of strawberries which realized a value over $800; 60 tons of hay which, including an oat crop cut when green, was harvested; 150 bushel of onions, which was an excellent crop of the best quality, the present quotation being $1.50 per bushel wholesale.

Also produced along with 100 bushels of rutabagas were 500 bushels of potatoes. Mr. Nourse has discovered in his experience in growing potatoes that the best results can be had by cultivating the White Rose or Beauty of Hebron varieties. Burbank's are found to be late coming to maturity and ran out sooner than other grades. He also had 15,000 head of salable cabbage which realized $20 per ton. A small average of carrots, beets, squash and musk melons of an excellent quality were also raised. A good supply of sweet corn was sent to Washburn and Bayfield during the season. A wagon load of vegetables is sent to Washburn and Bayfield twice a week and finds ready sale this fall. It must be understood that there is only a small acreage of the farm under cultivation and the results accruing from Mr. Nourse's enterprise and industry has been very satisfactory.

One of the most improved hay presses is in use on the farm which is sent throughout the county where ever its services are required. To show its capacity, not many days ago it baled for Mr. Pike of Bayfield 10 tons of hay in less than seven hours; 100 tons of hay was also put up in bale for Frank Stark in a short time. From a small acreage of clover two crops have been cut this season and that present a fair third crop is in sight. Mr. Nourse pre-meditates in the near future to go into raising hogs on clover and roots. He is of the opinion that pork can be grown to good advantage on clover pasturage and will meet with satisfactory financial results. A root house was built in a ravine which is capable of storing 5000 bushels of roots. The stock on the farm consists of five horses and four cows. An icehouse is one of the farm buildings and a good stock of ice is put up for use during the berry season and otherwise.

He has let a contract for the clearing of 25 acres this fall which he purposes breaking up next spring and asserts if he is blessed with good health in the course of a few years he will have a model farm and one that will compare to any in the state. The farm is beautifully located on a living spring. Close to the buildings on Onion River, a trout stream well known to local anglers meanders through the property. Suffice it to say that those who doubt the fertility of Bayfield County soil have only to visit this farm when their doubts will be cast to the wind and they will be convinced that agricultural pursuit in this county will be a leading feature in the future.

July 6, 1911 *Bayfield Progress*, "The State Experimental Farm adjoins Mr. Syke's place and here we found a crew of berry pickers hard at work. The experimental farm was designed principally for the purpose of experimenting with orcharding, but the land between the rows of young trees is being utilized for strawberry culture and the scheme apparently works fine. The trees are set twenty feet apart each way, which gives ample room for three rows of berries between each row of trees. The soil here is quite stiff clay, but on the cultivated plots it worked up mellow and had a good tilth. This was due largely to the fact that a great deal of humus was added to the soil previous to the planting of strawberries by turning under a heavy crop of green pea vines.

About twenty acres are planted to fruit trees and they include cherries of several varieties, plums, and apples both crab and large. Each row is plainly marked with the name of the variety, giving the visitors an opportunity to readily compare the various varieties insofar as they are able to determine by the appearance of the growing tree. All the trees were, of course, pruned in good shape, and thoroughly cultivated about. Not a sign of weeds or grass were to be found around them. We noticed that they were being kept sprayed with a germicide composed of lime, sulfur and water. The barks of the trees and their general appearance were faultless and their growth was all that could be desired for their age. They are not yet in bearing, that is, with a few exceptions, and about next year they will commence to make a return on the investment. Extracts from *Iron River Pioneer* inserted into the *Bayfield Progress*.

Harvey Nourse Sr. at the Pikes Creek Home site
BHA Pike Research Center Archive Collection

Chapter Five
Tourism & Boomtown Bayfield

The Harbor City's "Fabulous" Island View Hotel
BHA Pike Research Center Archive Collection

P. W. Smith's Hotel

Bayfield County Press - February 04, 1903

BHA Pike Research Center Archive Collection

Bayfield's Landmark Hostelries

Arranged by Robert J. Nelson

Celebrities Mary Todd-Lincoln, Union Civil War Generals William T. Sherman, George W. Morgan, Colonel T. L. Alexander of the U.S. Army, author and humorist Mark Twain and wife Olivia Langdon Clemons are all documented as port arrivals. Congressmen, Senators, Wisconsin Central and Omaha line railroad executives, speculators, showmen, circus men and con-men, Chautauqua promoters, baseball and lacrosse teams, opera singers and musical troupes arrived to Bayfield starting in the summer of 1856 and stayed and rented rooms in the local hostelries. From June to mid-September tourists migrated to the Harbor City for relaxation, natural beauty of the Apostle Islands and as an "air haven" relief center from Midwest hayfever symptoms and inter-city coal-fired smog and polluted air settings that permeated urban areas of the great lakes.

Well orchestrated advertisement campaigns worked. Day tourists and vacationers played, gamed and stayed at magnificent, five-star comparable hostelries. Under brightly lit chandeliers benefits were held, posh dinners served, libations offered in diminutive crystal champagne glasses or mugs of beer were drafted from kegs shipped from Milwaukee breweries. A tonsorial parlor barbered and groomed the moneyed for who the grand hotels were intended. Local patrons were also welcomed with open arms and attended grandiose masquerade balls, Valentine's Day, Christmas and New Years Eve parties. Independence Day celebrations with gunny-sack and row boat races intermingled with featured Lacrosse games between the Bad River and Chippewa nation athletes drew large crowds. Dancing from dark to dawn, "tripping the light fandango", concluded festivities in grand ballrooms. All was well in Camelot, but alas, all good situations come to pass.

By 1900 the once popular packet-boat and excursion boat operations wealthier clientele chose for travel purpose were on the wane. The Omaha Line railroad steam engines that once pulled luxurious Pullman coach cars to town became more of utilitarian nature. Clientele quickly changed from upper class travelers to working class business owners and laborers, entrepreneurs and emigrants seeking the great American Dream. The forthcoming narratives present the rise and fall of the "Golden Age" of the Harbor City's innkeeper and commerce industry.

The Smith Hotel was first constructed in 1856 by John B. Bono and a man named Resaue and was conducted by Bono under the name, the Bayfield Exchange. In 1862 this building exchanged hands to Captain Smith and was conducted by him almost continuously until the date of its destruction by fire in 1883. In its time the "Smith" entertained noteworthy men from of all parts of the Country; Vice Presidents, State Senators, members of Congress, noted army and navy officers and a host of seekers after good health and recreation. Here leading men from the South and East discussed grave questions of state and gloated over the trophies of their skill with rod and gun. Fair women and brave men have "tripped the light fantastic" in its spacious parlors. Now, like the great majority of guests, it is a thing of the past. Other buildings now stand upon its site and naught remains of the old-time glory but the cold representation shown above." *Bayfield County Press*, February 4, 1903

On December 25, a large hotel was commenced by the Bayfield Land Company [near the present day Presbyterian Church] and was finished in June, 1857. It was opened by Mr. Joseph Harvey Nourse and succeeded by Mr. George D. Livingstone as proprietor. On January 10, 1861 the building was totally destroyed by fire. John B. Bono opened the first hotel in the place on the corner now occupied by Duffy Boutin's saloon. In 1862 Captain Paul W. Smith bought the hotel of Mr. Bono, improved and enlarged it, until it covered the entire front of the block with the exception of a small yard at the alley which was almost entirely taken up by a fountain, made most attractive to strangers by its quantity of brook trout. The Smith Hotel and Captain Smith were widely known and during the twenty-five years of its existence, sheltered many of the prominent men of our country. In 1874 Mr. William Knight ran the hotel for six months. It burned in June 1877. Lillian-Tate Wilkinson, *Bayfield County Press*, March 24, 1904

In the *Ashland Daily Press* of September 27, 1947, Harvey Nourse, son of the afore-mentioned J. H. Nourse, was now living at Salmo, Wisconsin, a small community located south of Bayfield by the Bayfield fish hatchery. At this time he was known to be the oldest settler in the Chequamegon region and was a guest speaker at the 1947 gathering of the Chequamegon Bay Old Settlers' Club gathering. Harvey Nourse went on to say, "my father came to Bayfield in 1856. He was employed to manage a large hotel built on the hill where the Presbyterian Church now stands. This hotel burned shortly after. There were good hotels in Bayfield at that time, the oldest being the Smith Hotel, which burned and there was the Island View Hotel, run by Charlie Willey, which also burned, but was rebuilt. There also were some splendid boarding houses such as the LaBonte House by Nazaire LaBonte and the Fountain House run by Mrs. Boneo (aka Bono). The tourists delighted in staying at these places for they served such wonderful meals."

The Harbor City to this day has remained a tourist destination. Here presented is a short history of the pioneer tourism trade and fine hostelries in operation over one hundred years ago. The first Island View Hotel is the lead story from the golden age of innkeepers.

Original Island View Hotel
BHA Pike Research Center Archive Collection

The newspaper photo above was presented in the January 24, 1885 edition of the Bayfield County Press. Earliest on, the Island View Hotel was given the name Endaian Hotel, then Vaughn Hotel, and later re-named the "Island View House" by first owners, Sam and Mary Vaughn. Constructed in 1883, the landmark hostelry burned to the ground on April 4, 1887. This version of the Island View Hotel was located on the corner of Washington Avenue and First Street, Block 72, and appears as on lots 9-10 & 19-20.

In addition to the Bayfield Exchange, Smith House and Island View Hotels, many a unique hostelry crammed the streets of the Harbor City and need be mentioned; the Bayfield Inn, the Bayfield House-Hokenson and Anderson proprietors, Bracken Inn as per proprietor Bert Bracken, the German House, La Bonte House, Mrs. Frank Shaw's Lake Superior House on 1st Street, Lake View House, Pageant Inn, Union House, St. James Inn, Pat Howley's Boarding House and Inn, the Herbert House, the Parks Hotel and "Dad and Ma" Davis's- Davis House on Rittenhouse and Broad Street (April 23, 1893, *Bayfield County Press*), are among the documented. The Fountain House was built as a home, not as a hotel in 1856 by Antoine Bardon, who first occupied it. It was not opened as a hotel until 1877, which was by John B. Bono, the then proprietor.

The Harbor City, also named "Fountain City", was promoted vigorously locally and regionally to fill the hotels from June through September. To do so Editor and Publisher- Currie Bell gladly accommodated the innkeepers via the talented and stimulated pens of the local editorial staffs. In addition to boldly declaring, "Sail and picnic throughout the glorious Apostle Islands", "Come for the wonderful Speckled Brook Trout and shoreline rock fishing", "Visit the Government Observatory", etc.

Advertisements for the specialized customer to come to Bayfield for the 'fresh, clean air" theme certainly were in vogue and caught the eyes of readership living in the coal smoked industrial cities the likes of Chicago, Buffalo, St. Louis and Detroit. And play the "air-haven" theme heavily Bell did, year after year, in snippets like the following, "Mrs. A. A. Johnston who has been spending the hay fever season here, the guest of Mrs. Currie G. Bell returned to her home in Downers Grove, Illinois. This is a second season she has spent here and has returned home both seasons with her health very much improved. As a summer resort Bayfield is beautifully and fortunately located, and as a resort for hay fever sufferers too much in our favor cannot be said. The air, whether coming from the forest of pine that lie south and west, or off the cool waters of the great lake that stretches northward and eastward, is bracing, and has just the qualities necessary to tone up a tired body. If you come once you'll surely come again," *Bayfield County Press* October 2, 1897.

All marketing strategies worked well; Bayfield was a destination for the who's who of America. Showcased here is the most grand of hostelries the village could offer; the genesis of the Island View Hotel begins here.

Advertisements in the Bayfield County Press, July 7th, 1883
BHA Pike Research Center Archive Collection

Open for Business; The Endaian Hotel

Bayfield County Press – July 10, 1883

The *Press* noted that "work on Vaughn Hotel is about completed and next Tuesday, July 10, 1883 it will be opened by one of the finest balls ever given in this section of the country. This hotel is an institution in which each citizen of the Harbor City should have a lively interest, and now that it is to be thrown open to the public under competent management they should manifest an interest in it by attending this, its opening ball."

A few days later the Vaughn family must have second thoughts about the naming the structure with their name tied to it and re-christened it to be called, "the Endaian", an Indian word meaning "our home."

The opening ball at the new hotel was all that was promoted, "by the most sanguine save in point of numbers, and in this respect the crowd was fully ample for an enjoyable time. The large dining room had been cleared of its furniture and converted into a ballroom with well waxed floors, the polish of which was fully demonstrated on by more than one gay gallant. The music for the occasion was furnished by the Chequamegon Band and gave the best satisfaction, while the menu prepared under the watchful eye of that prince of caterers, Charlie Willey, gave ample evidence of the fact that the guest of his house would never have cause to complain in that direction. In the neighborhood of 30 couples came over from Ashland on the *S. B. Barker*, and remained until morning to convey them to their homes. To say that all unite in pronouncing it one of the most successful events of the kind ever given in the place is but, we believe, to speak the truth."

The August 4, 1883 *Bayfield County Press* stated that the "Endaian House" had been rechristened the "Island View House", a much more appropriate name, and by October 23 this same year settled in with the "Island View Hotel". Hereafter is a chronological order of events.

Tuesday July 10, 1883: first arrivals at the Endaian from Bayfield were: Robert Inglis; T. L. Patterson, wife and daughter; J. D. Cruttenden and wife; D. J. Cooper; George S. Green; Alonzo Knight; Orlando Flanders; Joseph Boutin; James Chapman; Curry G. Bell, Solomon D. Boutin; Isaac H. Wing; J. W. Remington; P. E. Brown and wife; Andrew Tate: William J Herbert; Captain Nils Larsen; T. A. Lang; Mrs. I. R. Harbert; Mrs. John McCloud; B. B. Wade; J. W. Atwood; Robinson D. Pike; N. I Willey – St. Paul.

From Ashland came: Dr. N. Booth; J. H. Doesburg; C. M. Davis; M. D. Woodruff; R. McKenny; John Stevens, E. A. Hayes, J. O Hayes ; M. W. Tompkins; L. T. Gregory; H. Richard; Mrs. F. Smith; N. D. Moore; C. J. Higgins and lady.

Out of Town guests included: Walter N. Leslie – Newcastle, Pennsylvania; C. D. Ti Linglast (sic) – Bloomer, Wisconsin; T. H. Wolford – Eau Claire; R. Ortman; J. A. Faulkner of Duluth; H. Norwood – Richmond, Virginia; F. W. Denison – Chicago; Thomas Ramsey – Detroit, Michigan; P. F. Kelly – Laverne, Michigan; J. M. Bingham – Chippewa Falls; S. R. Holden – Watkins Glen, New York; G. A. Ishbell and W. M. Pock – Ann Arbor, Michigan; F. H. Weir – Laporte, Indiana; Mrs. F. J. Bowman and daughter – St. Louis, Missouri; J. E. Harney; O.B. Hamlin, F. H. Peabody – Chicago; Charles Ward – Greenville Michigan; T. S. Kimball and wife – New York; J. E. Iverson Milwaukee; A. Frobach – Milwaukee.

October 20, 1883: Willey and Son, proprietors of the Island View House, are contemplating the erection of a large addition to their hotel and expect to have it completed by the opening of next season.

October 3, 1885: The number of guests registered at the Island View from June 1st to September 30 was 2176.

Fire & Resurrection

Bayfield County Press - April 9, 1887

Business was thriving at the Island View House, all was in order and then;

On the morning of April 4, 1886 at about 3:30 or so citizens were aroused by the cry of "fire!" It did not take long for those living on the flat to discover that the Island View Hotel was on fire and a general turnout was the order of the morning. The fire had caught in the kitchen and was rapidly spreading to the main building. A strong wind was blowing from the Northeast and the entire block with perhaps all of buildings south of the hotel to the lake were threatened. It was apparent to all that with the limited means at hand it would be impossible to save the hotel and the efforts of all were directed to the adjoining property. Two things averted a general conflagration, the snow which had fallen and been cursed by all the day before, and the hydraulic service. By six o'clock the hotel was burned to the ground.

The Island View was opened to the public in the summer of 1883 under the proprietorship of Willey & Son, the present proprietors. The building was insured for $6000 and was owned by Mrs. Vaughn, of Ashland. Furniture was insured for $1000. The estimated loss is at $4000, although it would be difficult to figure what the loss to their business will be as this is the most unfavorable time in the year for such an occurrence. They have already begun to fit up their property on the adjoining hill, formerly known as the Annex, by the addition of the kitchen and other conveniences and will be ready for the transient customer in a few days. It is the hope they will see their way clear to extensive enlargements of the present accommodations.

This fire has demonstrated several important facts. First, few places can boast of as many citizens proportion to size that will turn out and work with a will as Bayfield. Secondly, the inefficiency of our waterworks as compared with large cities has often been a cause of remark. Still with the improvements recently inaugurated they fulfill all present requirements. Thirdly, an efficient fire department is a necessity. No one denies but what the main portion of the hotel could have been saved had there been a trained fire department or someone to direct proceedings.

The Grand "Island View" Hotel Circa 1900
Elvis & Marguerite Moe Family Collection

A Silver Lining Behind Every Cloud

Arranged by Robert J. Nelson

"Passing of the Island View will be fare-you-well to the last of the great summer resort hotels. A quarter century ago such hostelries were springing up here, there and everywhere where lay an attractive expanse of water. They catered especially to the very wealthy. Their rates were the only observable evidence of the high cost of living of that period; but they gave to their patrons chance for summer rest amidst pleasing surroundings, they served good fare in high-class manner and their attached buffets and gambling quarters afforded excitement to the fashionable bases who flocked from the cities.

But change came to the taste of mortals, and these big summer hotels went out of fashion. During the last fifteen years hardly a one has been erected in the entire land, and one by one such as had been builded have retired from use or torn down. Today the family which is over burdened with money will hunt out a lake shore site or ocean coast promontory and build thereon a palace of its own. If coin be not so plentiful, but desire and opportunity for summer leisure is strong, a summer cottage of less or greater modesty will serve. But in modern times it's nix on the big summer hotel. The rich won't make 'em pay; the less wealthy cannot afford to patronize them. *Bayfield County Press*, October 16, 1916

Now starts a chronological order of eventswhich chronicles the construction of the new Island View Hotel - #2. The headlines of the Bayfield County Press on April 16, 1887 boldly stated that a

Fine New Hotel Costing Upwards of $10,000 would rise in the Harbor City and would *Afford Better Accommodation and Offer More Attractions to Summer Tourists. The Work Will Be Pushed with Vigor.*

Steadfast Island View Hotel supporter, mover and shaker Currie G. Bell, suggests the following blueprint to success at the old Town Hall. "At the meeting held last Saturday evening to raise money to build a new hotel in place of the Island View, enough was subscribed towards the commencement of the work, and ere many days roll by ground will be broken for the erection of a fine new hotel to cost about $10,000. The new building will be built on the corner of Washington Avenue and First Street, across the avenue from the old building, and will be connected with the Annex on the hill, thus supporting one of the finest sites in this section, overlooking the beautiful scenery of Chequamegon Bay and the far famed Apostle Islands.

The office, wash room, sample rooms, will be on the lower floor. The parlors, dining room and so forth, will be on the second floor, the same as the old building. It will be furnished with all modern conveniences, such as telephone service, electric bells, and bathrooms with hot and cold water and the building throughout will be lighted by electricity or gas. The exact dimensions of the hotel are not definitely known at this early writing, the plans not having been completed, but it will contain in the neighborhood of 100 rooms and will thus afford ample accommodations for at least 200 guests. The rooms will all be well ventilated, of convenient size, and furnished in the best style. No pains will be spared in the building of this new hotel to serve the wants and desires of the guests we are of good fortune it may be they to visit it. In fact, it will be constructed with an eye to please the most critical, and when completed Bayfield can justly boast of the model hotel of this size in this section of the country.

It is confidently expected, and in fact it can be stated beyond a doubt that the new building will be completed and ready for reception of the guests by July 1, 1887. The Harbor City, which is a favorite resort for so many summer tourists, will thus afford better accommodations than ever to these annual visitors and the *Press* firmly believes that the coming season will witness such an influx of tourists as Bayfield has never had before. Thus it seems that the burning of the old Island View which was thought at the time to be such a calamity will result in providing the Harbor City with just the kind of hotel it demands, and the dark cloud of two weeks ago may yet possess a silver lining."

April 16, 1887: Willey and Son are ready to entertain guests in the annex on the hill. *Bayfield County Press*

By May 28, 1887 the new Island View is in the process of construction and has a frontage on First Street of 160 feet, and on Washington Avenue of 120 feet. The new part is four stories high and the Annex two stories. When completed it will undoubtedly be the finest hotel on Lake Superior for summer resort purposes. It is to be supplied with pure soft spring water, electric bells and telephone service. Get ready for the grand opening of the Island View Hotel. Date about July 1.

As noted in the *Press* of July 9, 1887, "Bayfield's mammoth new summer resort hotel will now to be formally opened to the public by a grand ball and banquet. The *Press* intends at this time to present its readers with a view of this model structure, but owing to unavoidable circumstances finds it impossible. A pen and ink description is always unsatisfactory, no matter how well it may be done, unless accompanied by an illustration of the image described; hence when you have read the following brief description close your eyes and let your imagination dream of the handsome little town nestling beneath romantic bluffs, its streets lined with lovely shade trees, sparkling fountains of pure spring water and many a grassy lawn, wide and well-kept walks and at its feet the blue waters of that grandest of lakes, while in the distance, "like gems of living green" lies the far famed Apostle Islands.

Within a stone's throw of the beach, perched upon a beautiful plateau overlooking town, the bay and islands is an ornamental structure of magnificent proportions, surrounded by spacious verandas, the very appearance inviting to all in search of rest and comfort. Gaze upon its exterior proportions with a frontage on the east of 160 feet and on the south 120 feet. Walk in through its spacious portals and view its elegantly hardwood furnished office 40' x 40', in a cool and airy dining hall 44 x 68', it's grand parlor 23 x 53'; scroll through its roomy halls and see every hamlet, airy, well ventilated rooms; it's bathroom toilets on every floor – all these and many other striking features are sure to attract your attention and excite favorable comment, and you'll be led to exclaim, this is the place I long have sought, and mourned because I found it not!" *Bayfield County Press*

Years of moderate success pass, time has taken a toll on the struggling inn and the hotel shuts it doors temporarily. On April 17, 1903, the headlines turn to the positive and announce, *Leased! Bayfield's Popular Hotel Will Be Opened: Bailey Takes Hold. Summer Guests Assured of First-Class Accommodations This Summer.*

Currie Bell writes to the column with an expressive truthfulness, "Lack of accommodations for several years past has forced many summer visitors to seek recreation in other fields. This now has been remedied; Bayfield's popular hotel will be open this summer, and all who will come may do so with the assurance that accommodations of first-class will be in the waiting. Yesterday J. C. Bailey, present proprietor of the Parks Hotel in town, leased the Island View for one year, with the privilege of three, and will at once commence getting it in shape for summer guests and the public in general.

This place has been closed for some time and that has greatly interfered with the tourist afflicted with the Bayfield fever. That the summer trade will be greatly increased by the opening of this hotel there is no doubt, and the people here see nothing but success in the undertaking. Now for a prosperous summer! Take your hat is off to J. C."

The master journalist further reports in September of 1903 that "repair work at the Island View Hotel has been going on for some time and in another week J. C. Bailey, proprietor of the Hotel Parks, expects to be located therein. The building was in a very dilapidated condition when Mr. Bailey leased it last spring and no attempt has been made the past summer to put the same in shape for the accommodation of guests. In the past few weeks however, some great changes have been wrought in the appearance of the building inside. In the first place, Mr. Bailey ordered two furnaces and the same are here and now being put in. One of these will heat the dining room and parlor and the other the rooms and halls on the third floor. Coal will be used this winter and proprietor Bailey is firm that the mine workers will not get the strike fever.

The parlor has been carpeted and when furnished will make one of the prettiest and most comfortable rooms in the hotel. From the windows of the spacious rooms one may command a fine view of the lake. The office has been fixed up considerable and it is probable that the electric call bell system will be put in operation this fall. The dining room, the scene of many society events and the one in which hundreds of summer visitors have partaken of delicious meals, will be papered to a new effect, to be red. In the kitchen is where the greatest amount of work must be done. Carpenters are now at work in the kitchen and by tomorrow will have it in fairly good shape.

Mr. Bailey has been pressed for room all summer and it was necessary for him to fall back on accommodations in private families. Everything will be in first-class shape for the tourist season and that the opening of the place will be a paying proposition is no doubt. The famous Island View will be open to the public in less than two weeks and may its proprietor be ever successful."

Bell was feeling rather merry about the transition and new innkeeper as he reports, "It recalls old times to see life and activity at the Island View and the people of Bayfield should take their hats off to J. C. Bailey as he has volunteered to furnish the city with a first-class hotel. A town without a good a hotel is a dead one and I don't believe one ever existed that prospered under such circumstances."

The Island View is now open for business. Mr. Bailey had moved his hotel furnishings from the Parks Hotel the last week and was now fairly well settled. One of the furnaces had been put up and was now in working order and it was the way for the proprietor to show the public that both were ready for action and that this large building could be made very comfortable during the winter. The dining room had been papered in new and red colors and the first step over the threshold, claims Bell, "gives one an appetite. The electric call bell system will soon be put in shape. There still remains some papering to be done in the halls, but all this will come about in time and when the gentle spring rolls around J. C. will be prepared to accommodate all comers."

This short story of the time period in 1895 fills in a historical blank of these times of yore Bayfield building. "The Island View Hotel, opening June 1, seems to be the absorbing topic among our citizens at present. Well, it may be, as never before in its history has the Island View undergone such a thorough cleaning from top to bottom as this season. Mechanics of almost every class have been employed for weeks putting the hotel in thorough order, to say nothing of the army of scrub women. An average of seven rooms was cleaned per week, painting, calcimining, paper hanging, etc., as been done. New carpets, new china, glassware, table silverware, etc. to replace the old has been purchased. Colored male help will be an innovation. The day for waitresses at the Island View has passed. Not only are the colored men waiters but they are good musicians as well and it is the intention of the manager to have music every evening.

Every department of the hotel is presided over by old and experienced hotel men. Mr. E. E. Peck will have charge of the office; Mr. Harry Weeks of the storerooms and pantry; both these gentlemen hail from Chicago. Mr. LaRoque, from France, chef of the kitchen has no superior in this country, his record speaks for itself and his cooking this season will add to the laurels. Mr. LaRoque is ably assisted by his son Edmund. The services of Mrs. D'Vine, from Boston, have been secured as pastry cook. Miss Johnson, from Indian River Hotel, Rockledge, Florida, will have charge of the laundry; and last but not least Mr. Samuel C. Hough will do the stewarding in addition to filling the position as manager.

Mr. Hough brings to the hotel an experience of 20 years, part of the time as proprietor of some large hotels, namely the Pico House of Los Angeles California, 180 rooms. Mr. Hough furnished and opened the first hotel at Santa Monica, California which he sold out to take the "*Pico*." Last summer he was so unfortunate as to lose by fire not only his hotel at Pine Lake, Indiana but all that he possessed, watch, chain, books, etc. If experience, economy and close attention to business can make a hotel pay then we will in advance congratulate the stockholders of the *Island View Hotel*. We advise anyone that can place their names on the new hotel register Saturday and not take our say so, but sit down in the dining room and see what Mr. Hough can do in the way of catering to the inner man." *Bayfield County Press*, June 1, 1895

The *Washburn Times*, on September 14th of 1895, in an area report of the tourism trade, and especially the hostelry business, showed a business that year in a downward spiral. The *Times* says,

"The social season at Lake Superior resorts has been somewhat quieter than former years. While pleasure and excursion boats have been well patronized, it is noticeable that the number of summer tourists at the hotels is vastly less than in past years. Ashland's popular resort, the Chequamegon Hotel, has closed its dining room within the past week, owing to the small amount of business, and the Island View Hotel at Bayfield has done perceptibly less business than in other years. At Madeline Island there are a great many cottages and no small number are camping out in tents. Still, tourists are not plentiful as in past years - no doubt owing to the depression in the industrial and commercial world.

Prior, on September 7, 1895 in an "items of interest" column from LaPointe in the *Press* the scribe reported that the summer cottage and campers had nearly all departed but the Island's Park Hotel still kept as guests a "nice compliment" of renters. "Perch will be served from the Island Park tonight", spoke an ad in this version of *Bayfield County Press.*

An Old Legend Comes to Pass

Bayfield Progress - October 16, 1916

Bayfield's rendition of the Waldorf Astoria, the pride of the Harbor City, the Island View Hotel, meeting the fate of so many a fine hostelry of the roaring 1890s came to conclusion in a not so dignified sequences of events. The *Bayfield Progress* offers the swan song and finale of the once great institution of tourism destinations.

The Island View Hotel building is very shortly to disappear from the face of the local landscape. It was purchased Monday by A. H. Wilkinson from William Werder, the Ashland man who has long been its owner. Mr. Wilkinson will have the structure razed this fall, and the lumber, most of which is of such quality as is not now-a-days readily obtainable, is being saved with care for building purposes.

For twenty-five years this building has been a landmark on this coast. Time was when it hummed with activity from June to October of each year, guests coming by the scores and by hundreds from great lake ports and from cities inland, to people seeking rooms during the hot months. Its flaunting flag by day, its brilliant lights by night greeted travelers via the waters, and men and women of wide prominence were annual guests under its roof. But suddenly, in obedience to command and to pressure from the then all-powerful railroad combinations, the packet-boat service was withdrawn from this port and the Island View hostelry fell promptly into disuse. Persistent attempts were made thereafter to operate it; but it could never be made to pay expenses. Travel via the lake went straight from the Soo to Duluth without intermediate stops and tourists who came via rail found equal comforts at lesser cost in the smaller hotels, — either that, or they built summer cottages of their own on the mainland or islands and were independent of a landlord. The passing of the Island View will ring the curtain on the last of these great hostelries on Lake Superior. Incidentally, it will take from the local landscape a structure which has become pretty much an eyesore."

Christopher Columbus tied to the North Dock
September 27, 1897

BHA Pike Research Center Archive Collection

Christopher Columbus – Popular Excursion Steamer

Bayfield County Press - Saturday, June 26, 1897

Many a steamer transit liner hooked tie lines to Bayfield's North dock from the 1880s through 1900. One such craft was the whaleback *Christopher Columbus*, yard number 00128. Commissioned for construction by the World's Fair Steamship Company in 1892 and built by the American Steel Barge Company between 1892 and 1893 at Superior, Wisconsin, the *Chris* would steam twice to Bayfield in 97 to show off her whiteness, company colors and deliver fare-paying patrons out for a joy ride.

Distinguished from all other whalebacks by her white coat of paint, the *Chris* toured the great lakes until 1933. Later morphed into a Great Lakes excursion liner, the *Chris* was one of many whalebacks but is the only ship of her kind ever built exclusively for passenger service. The ship was designed by developer and promoter Alexander McDougall and is listed as 362 feet in length; her cost $360,000. Father Time's daughter Demise visited her hull over the years and in 1936 at Manitowoc Shipbuilding Company - Manitowoc, Wisconsin the state-of-the-art great lakes liner was scuttled.

Although her trips to the Harbor City were few and far between, the two times documented she touched base certainly were colorful experiences for the paying patrons. The following articles describe her exploits of her days in Bayfield. The *Superior Leader* had the following to say about a June day excursion in 1897 in which the *Chris* journeyed her course to Bayfield. Entered in the columns of the *Bayfield County Press*, the headlines read, *"Brings two immense excursions here from Duluth and Superior"* and *"Over 5000 people here last Saturday and Sunday"*. Then comes the tale of September 19th.

Last Saturday and Sunday were two gala days for Bayfield. Fully five thousand people visited the Harbor City. Last Saturday was the first trip that the *Christopher Columbus* made this season, and it was a grand success.

The big excursion steamer yesterday carried 1600 passengers from the head of the lakes to the Apostle Islands and Bayfield, and there was not a single incident during the whole trip to mar the pleasure of the excursionists. The weather was warm and the lake was like glass for the greater part of the voyage. Good music and dancing was had in the cabin, and plenty of refreshments topped off the pleasures of the trip. The *Christopher* left the ship yard at nine o'clock yesterday morning with over 300 Superiorites on board, at Duluth they took on nearly 1000 cliff dwellers; then on the way down a run was taken into Two Harbors and 300 more pleasure seekers were added to the list. The crowd found plenty to amuse them during the trip over to the Apostle Islands, watching lake crafts, dancing and promenading the deck. When passing through the islands, the scenery occupied the attention of all. They ran into Bayfield and stayed there for an hour and then took up the trip home.

The *Christopher* arrived here, at midnight, being three hours off the scheduled time. This was caused by the fact that it was her first trip this year and Captain Smith did not care to put the big whaleback to a test so early in the season. The Superior contingent seemed to enjoy the delay. They all agreed that they had a good time, and praised the management for the way they conducted the trip."

Sunday was another beautiful day and the *Christopher's* second trip was an immense success. She arrived in Bayfield about three o'clock in the afternoon with about 3000 excursionists on board. She remained at the dock one hour, giving the people plenty of time for a stroll around town, which they hugely enjoyed after being on the boat most of the day.

The steamer *Hunter*(1) arrived from Two Harbors just ahead of the *Christopher* with a large crowd on board. The *Plowboy* and the *Fashion* both run excursions from Ashland, making in all four excursions to Bayfield in one day.

Bayfield is to be congratulated on being the only town on Chequamegon Bay which has had the honor thus far of welcoming that magnificent steamer, *Christopher Columbus*, to her port.

Here's what the *Duluth News Tribune* says about the excursion Sunday; "the excursion yesterday under the auspices of the Grocers Association was a great success. The *Christopher Columbus* took about 2500 people from Duluth and Superior over the shining bosom of Gitchie Gumme to Bayfield and back.

The start was made about 10AM when the famous whaleback arrived at the foot of Fifth Avenue West and almost 2000 people boarded her at that point. A belated passenger attempted to board the boat just outside the canal, and much to the somewhat cruel amusement of the excursionists, he succeeded only in getting a complete ducking.

No stop was made at Two Harbors, but the run to Raspberry Island light was a perfect dream of calm water sailing. There the picturesque sail through the Apostle Islands began. Every lighthouse was saluted by the big, hoarse whistle of the *Christopher Columbus*, and duly responded to by "dipping" the colors three times that were flying at each government station.

Bayfield, the objective point of the trip, was reached about 3 PM. The whole population, apparently of this exceedingly pretty little town was on the dock to greet the *Christopher Columbus*, and her reverberant whistle, mingled with the music of the Duluth City Band and the cheers of the citizens of Bayfield.

Port Collector Inglis, a lifetime friend of Captain Bob Smith, promptly gave the steamboat a clearance, and the crowd scattered around the romantic old settlement on a 45 minutes' leave. At four promptly the whistle called "all aboard" and almost all responded. An unfortunate Duluth businessman gallantly threw his overcoat in the water, and then lacked the nerve to make a jump for the departing steamboat. The run home to Duluth was idyllic." (End)

After scoring highly with tourists of the first successful event, the *SS Christopher Columbus* returned to Bayfield for a second rendezvous, recorded in the *Bayfield County Press* of September 25, 1897 in article entitled, *"Balloon Went Up." "Professor Deer Made a Successful Ascension from the Deck of the Christopher Columbus* read the headlines this day. The two largest crowds that ever visited Bayfield were landed here last Saturday and Sunday by the big whaleback steamer *Christopher Columbus*. Fully 8000 excursionists visited the Harbor City. Sunday was the last trip for the *Christopher* and closed the most successful season in her experience. Here told is the rest of that colorful adventure.

On Saturday the *Christopher* landed at the Dalrymple dock with over 2000 people on board. She remained at the dock one hour, during which time the excursionists took in the sights of the town.

Professor Deer made an attempt at balloon ascension while in the harbor. The balloon was held on the windward side by 15 or 20 men, but when two thirds inflated a heavy gust of wind caught it piling up the men in a heap, the boom swept the deck, knocking over the hot air flue and set it on fire. The men immediately let go of the guy ropes and the large airship blew over into the water where the flames were extinguished. Considerable excitement prevailed, causing two ladies to faint, fortunately no one was injured.

Here is what the *Superior Evening Telegram* has to say of the excursion: "Sunday's excursion was a success. While the weather was cold there was a lesson on Saturday and the scenes of hundreds of people leaning over the railings, ostensibly to look at the water were not repeated. On Saturday the crowd got sick by the hundreds. Many did not enjoy the trip on this account and lunch baskets were not touched. About 4000 people were on the excursion of Saturday and the same number Sunday.

The balloon ascension was of course one of the principal attractions. On Saturday several attempts were made to raise the affair, the last one being at Bayfield. There a gust of wind took a fall out of the airship and a big hole was accidentally burned in the canvas which leaned the balloon up for repairs. Sunday the airship was repaired, and when the *Christopher* was lying at the dock at Bayfield during our stop, the ascension was made. The balloon was inflated with hot air upon the forward deck, and an additional staff being erected to hold a canvas in place during the process. It took about fifteen minutes to inflate the balloon as a dozen men held her down as the constantly increasing size doubled efforts to get away.

Suddenly there was a signal. The men on the guy ropes released their hold and the balloon shot upward. It was one of the prettiest aeronautic performances ever seen. Suspended from the bottom of the balloon proper was a parachute. Suspended from the parachute was the trapeze, and as the balloon left the deck at the rate of a mile in about eleven seconds, Professor Patsy G. Deer was seen hanging by his feet from the bar. An instant later he reversed his position and held on by his teeth.

It seemed an incredibly short time but the balloon was up in the air between 3000 and 4000 feet when the professor pulled a string and let the parachute off. Down it shot with the professor dangling at the trapeze. Inside of three hundred feet the parachute opened like a huge white canvas umbrella and swung slowly down to terra firma. A good many people thought the dissent even at this was too fast for comfort. Professor Deer landed a few hundred feet back from the lake in Bayfield, safe and sound.

The balloon, now the size of a hen's egg, was rapidly emptying its hot air. Relieved of the weight which had kept the opening below; it turned bottom up and came down in the top of some trees. Ten seamen from the *Chris* were waiting for it and picked it up, bringing it on shipboard and the vessel immediately pulled away.

The *Columbus* stopped Sunday at Two Harbors, Minnesota and took on a good crowd from there. Duluth was left at 10:30 and Two Harbors was reached at noon. At four o'clock they were at Bayfield and left there at 5 PM. The day despite its coldness was pleasant. The South Superior Band on board furnished music and the big main cabin was filled to overflowing at all times. The big crowds carried by the *Chris* demonstrate that she is easily the most popular excursion steamer on the lakes. She goes into winter quarters at the Barge Company's plant in Superior and preparations are now being made to lay her up until next spring.

Full Ahead – Full Astern
Christopher Columbus: September 19, 1897
BHA Pike Research Center Archive Collection

(1) The steamer *Hunter* at this point in time was making daily trips to Duluth and all the South Shore points and had been meeting with great success and was greatly appreciated by the traveling public. The "Hunter" is a "fast, safe and first-class boat, and has the best of accommodations and good sleeping berths. Captain Clausen, who was in command was considered one of the most experienced men that ever sailed on the lake, and all those that sail with him can be sure of the safe and pleasant trip", said the *Ashland Press* on June 26, 1897.

Chapter Six
The Iron Horse Arrives

The Bayfield Scoot
BHA Pike Research Center Archive Collection

Bayfield Depot on Manypenny Avenue Circa 1890s
BHA Pike Research Center Archive Collection

Are We to Get a Railroad?

Are We to Get a Railroad? The Legislature has finally passed an act exempting the lands of the *St. Croix Land Grant*, lying in Ashland and Bayfield counties, from taxation for five years. After, they shall be acquired by a company that will build the road, providing twenty miles that on this end is constructed within two years.

Without this exemption, it would have been entirely fruitless to have made any efforts to obtain the necessary capital to build the road, and it does not necessarily follow, nor is it by any means certain that the inducements offered by the exemption, that such capital can be had, yet it greatly encourages efforts to be put forward for it.

This exemption has not been obtained without an outlay of money and loss of time, and much excellent management by those who have been instrumental in getting the legislation. There was great opposition and disinclination to allow any such measure to become a law. It arose in consequence of the very great unpopularity of exempting property from its proportionate burdens of caring on government. This opposition was overcome in this case, by patient, diligent, discrete management. The measure itself commended itself, it is true, by its peculiar and exceptional merits, these could not have overcome the unpopularity of such legislation, nor save the act from going under the feet, without the valuable services which have been referred to.

And we take pleasure in calling attention to the fact that the people of this county are indebted to Bayfield's Isaac H. Wing, Esquire, who for six weeks has given his time, money and patience in securing this legislation. He went to Madison, inaugurated the movement, and has been constantly in attendance upon this measure for the last six weeks, which is likely to play such an important part to the future of this section of the state, and especially Bayfield County. It is also to be observed that Honorable Samuel S. Fifield has rendered valuable services in this matter, and he has been Mr. Wing's faithful and efficient lieutenant.

In addition to his efforts in getting this exemption bill passed, Mr. Wing has labored to get capital enlisted in the enterprise, and we have some reason to hope that these efforts have not been wholly unsuccessful. Whilst the sufficient amount of money has not been found yet, we hope that so good a portion is thought to be available that future efforts will result in complete success. It must not be thought or believed from this that there is a probability that the money can be had. Is such a thing barely possible, and in the present deranged condition of the finances, and widespread alarm that has ceased the capitalist, it would be a wonder if the money is obtained. We hope for the best.

Our town and county authorities are now charged with great responsibility, for the County will of necessity have to help this railroad project along, and if heavy taxes are to be imposed, and frittered away on unnecessary highways and other extravagant follies, it will be useless to move forward in further efforts to get a railroad. Every possible reduction should be made at County and Township expense – every improvement that can be possibly dispensed with ought to be brought out for existence and out of getting taxes levied to make them. Let us go along carefully, and then all our efforts to get a railroad will prevail. If we can get twenty miles rail from Bayfield South, in 1878, the St. Croix Railroad will be accomplished fact in three years. It can be done."

The Apostle Islands, 22 in number, lay at her feet in the placid waters of the bay, like so many diamonds; away and beyond them to the East, the vast expanse of the Gitchie Gumme, "The Big Seawater", was spread out before us as far as the vision could reach; to the north, the shoreline of the North Coast, with its range of hills was distinctly outlined; to the Southwest and unbroken forest of hardwood in Pine, in all its primeval grandeur, presented a panorama that overly dwarfs our feeble efforts to describe. The stately old pines of the best forest appeared like toy trees which children set up when Noah is put forth to watch animals emerging from the Ark. But, not more wooden are the ark animals of our childhood than the words in which man would cloth such as scene. "Put down your wooden bits bit by bit; throw in color here, a little shade there, touch it up with sky and cloud, cast about it the perfume of blossom or breeze, and in heavens name what does it come to after all? Can the I wander away, away, until this loss in the blue distance, as a lark is lost in blue heaven, but the site still drinks the beauty of the landscape, though the source of the beauty may be unseen, as the source of the music which falls from the azure depths of the sky." *Bayfield Press,* Wednesday, April 30, 1879

A New Railway to Bayfield

By Business Manager- Maurice Edwards

Bayfield Press - March 30, 1878

Building of the Chicago, St. Paul, Minneapolis and Omaha Railway (1), most often referred to as the Omaha, from Ashland Junction to Bayfield followed a series of chronological events. Currie G. Bell- Editor and Publisher of the *Bayfield County Press*, in attendance celebrating with local town folk the 27th anniversary of the founding of Bayfield wrote in his paper:

"Twenty-seven years, one week past, the first blow was struck and the first tree fallen on the site of the present Village of Fountains.(2) Twenty-seven years of patient waiting, hoping and praying for railroad communication with the outside world which was to result in causing Bayfield to bloom and blossom into a city of no mean proportions. Young men have grown old and old men have been laid in the silent city of the dead without seeing their hopes realized while another generation has sprung up to reap the reward of their labors. What shall the harvest be? Let alone cause Bayfield to bloom and blossom into a city? We fear not. Without it she has been a failure; with that, she will realize the fruition of the hopes of her founders, if our people so will it; but they have work to do – hard, earnest, practical, effective work. Work that to perform demands united and unselfish effort of all. The railroad is the lever that can be used to accomplish this much desired result. Will we use it or will we not?" March 31, 1883

Until October 12, 1883, 4:04 PM all travel and transportation to Bayfield was by water or on ice, by sailing rig, steamship, wagon, stagecoach or on foot. Appreciated for years was the sighting of Bayfield's spring supply ships arriving later April, i.e. *Independence*, *Mineral Rock* and *Manistee*. With the coal bin, staples, provisions and groceries running dangerously low, ship spotters sitting atop the old military observation tower (3) on the North hillside hustled to the nearest wharf where the details of the vessels spotted were broadcast as the steamer, breaking candled and float ice, rounded Grants' Point on Madeline Island and headed for the North dock.

In the pioneering time period of the Chequamegon Bay vicinity, early La Pointe residents of the 1840s and Bayfielder's from 1856 to 1883 were ice bound, often from December to April's end, and near land-locked. Fall time weather was wet and windy, winters long and arduous, springs wet and cold, summers- just tough sledding. Travel or product transport from the Harbor City by stagecoach or wagon over the ice with treacherous pressure cracks was menacing, or ferrying the *Eva Wadsworth* to catch a July 4th baseball game in the late 1870s at McClelland, now Washburn, or fix a winters ride to St. Paul for the Winter Carnival over the old Bayfield-St. Croix Trail were travel options. If one was inclined, as was the territory's first Legislator Asaph Whittlesey, one could snowshoe to Kilborn City in Juneau County, and then catch the *Wisconsin Central* railway to Madison for the session.

As the virgin pine lands were harvested and replaced by farmlands and communities in the New Wisconsin the railway system of travel was making its way north to the Harbor City area. In 1877 the Wisconsin Central Railroad from Milwaukee connected at Penokee Gap, meeting it's Ashland sister line, which had started it's course south in 1872. Ashland the "Garland City" now held the keys to the port shipping trades of white pine timber and iron ore from the Penokee Mountain range.

While Ashland had railroad service, Bayfield and Washburn would not unit 1883. The *Progress* expresses well the tone of the community as the Harbor City fathers for many a year begged and eagerly awaited a railway connection to the outside world as granted by authorization of land acquisition through the St. Croix Land Grant. Business manager Edwards introduces the concept and Isaac H. Wing, Bayfield's benevolent "mover and shaker". Here he brings the question to the people and the politician's table. Five years later, the final track spike would be pounded home at the Bayfield depot.

(1) The Northern Division line of the Omaha ran a course from St. Paul and Minneapolis through Northline, an unincorporated community near Hudson, Wisconsin, to Bayfield. At Spooner, Wisconsin the Eastern Division met the Northern, followed the track two miles north to Trego Junction. There the Omaha branched north toward Superior, Wisconsin and northeasterly toward Bayfield. Villages serviced along the Bayfield route were Hayward, Cable, Drummond, Grand View, Mason, entering into the Ashland Junction site and then east to Ashland, the Garland City, or northerly through Barksdale to Washburn, the Sawdust City, dead-heading at Bayfield.

(2) Along with the Harbor City title designation, Bayfield in her early days found flowing fountains originating from the Bayfield Creek watershed filled with Brook Trout in many a yard, thus the name "Fountain City" was also delegated as a nick-name.

(3) The old Observatory was placed into action by the United States Government circa the Civil War era. Honorable A. J. Turner describes the view from the "Old Observatory" at Bayfield, in the *Wisconsin State Register*. "Friday morning broke clear and beautiful. After breakfast the orders for the date were agreed upon. Mr.'s Isaac Wing and William Knight had most generously placed their magnificence boat at the disposal of our party. Oarsmen were engaged, and most of the party when coasting up and down the bay, the ladies enjoying their opportunities for collecting specimens. For ourselves we had a little different programme. With Professor Lawrence and a gentleman from St. Paul, we started for the Government Observatory, situated on the highest eminence of the hills back of Bayfield, three miles distant. An hour's brief walk brought us to the object we started for, and in a moment more we were at the top. What a view was presented.

Linked at Last

Editor- Currie G. Bell

Bayfield County Press - **Saturday, October 13, 1883**

"Ere this issue of the *Press* is read by our subscribers residing outside the Harbor City the first regular passenger train will have rolled into this village which for twenty-seven long years has waited so patiently for the arrival of the iron horse, the last blow of the hammer having fallen upon the golden spike that signaled the completion of this great enterprise inaugurated so long ago.

Friday, October 12 will ever remain a memorable date to the citizens of the Harbor City that being the date of the completion of this iron pathway to the outer world. On the morning of that day Conductor Hinckley's construction train was at Julius Austrian's clearing and he promised to have the track in and his train at the depot ere the setting of the sun. All day long the workmen were surrounded by an anxious throng of men, women and children, wrought up to a high pitch of excitement, and as the day wore on the track men and track layers seem to imbibe a portion of the spirit and redoubled their efforts as they touched toward their goal.

As the hands of the clock pointed to the hour, 4:04, the train halted in front of the depot, the *Star Spangled Banner* was flung to the breeze, the old brass cannon belched forth flame and smoke, the whistles of the various steam engines in the harbor united with those of the locomotive, and the bells of churches and schools in one prolonged salute that echoed from hilltop to hilltop, welled from the throats of these excited throngs, cheer after cheer. Its completion to the old pioneers who have waited so long for its arrival was like a dream more than a reality and they stand dazed in the light of their long-delayed good fortune.

The importance of this event to northern Wisconsin and the great west, as well as this immediate locality, is incalculable. It forms a grand highway from the rich plains of the far west to this inland seaport for which their products may find rapid and cheap transit to the markets of the East. It opens up and renders available to settlement a grand territory of valuable timberlands and gives outlet to the great pinaries of the northwestern part of the state, thus pioneering the way for the capitalist and the laborer to the rich fields for their enterprise and skill. It renders available for maritime business one of the grandest harbors in the world and its coming is hailed with rejoicing by the storm tossed mariner as well as by those who heralded its coming by settling upon its shores long years ago.

To attempt even a condensed history of this enterprise is out of the question, as time or space will not permit. However, it is a history with which our readers are more or less familiar and instead of dwelling upon that part fraught with so many bitter disappointments let us accept the fact of its completion with hopeful hearts and look to the goal of future for the reward of the weary years of the past.

A lesson: There is one point in the history of this great work that we may dwell upon with profit. And that is the fact that the railway completion is the result of a boundless faith in its ultimate success and a determination on the part of its projectors to push it to completion. A like manifestation of faith in the Harbor City by its founders and a like determination on the part of her citizens to push her to the front and make her the leading maritime port on the "great unsalted" may have a like result.

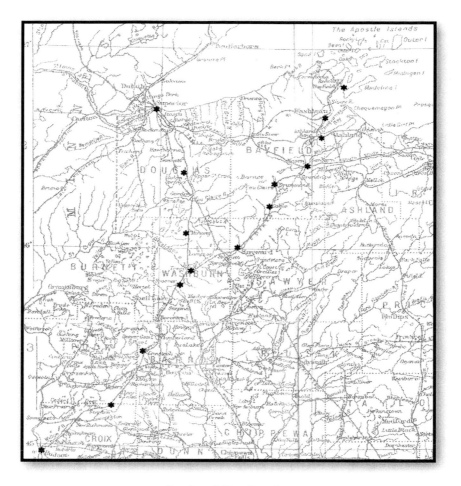

Route of the Omaha
Encyclopedia Britannica 1911 - Eleventh Edition

Robert J. Nelson Collection

The Royal Route
October 13, 1883

BHA Pike Research Center Archive Collection

Congratulation telegrams: Tuesday Superintendent H. C. Hope arrived in the village and proceeded to connect us with the outside world by telegraph. The company has the record that their telegraph line is in a very substantial manner and has two strong wires – one for the railroad and the other for commercial purposes. The first messages sent over the wires were as follows:

From Bayfield to:

- Henry M. Rice – "wire in and train expected Saturday. Shake. From Colonel J. (Joel) D. Cruttenden."

- C. D. O'Brien, Mayor of St. Paul – Bayfield, the Harbor City of Lake Superior, sends greetings to the Saintly City of the Northwest connected by wire this day.

- Mayor of Hudson Wisconsin – the Harbor City sends greetings to one of her warmest friends, the city of Hudson.

- Mayor of Minneapolis – the Harbor City of Lake Superior sends greeting to the queen of the Northwest.

- Board of Supervisors Superior – the Harbor City of Lake Superior greets you in Superior City.

- City of Milwaukee – Bayfield is in the state connected with the outside world by telegraph and regular trains will be running into the Harbor City Monday the 15th. She sends greetings to the "Cream City" and hopes for better acquaintance.

- Mayor of Duluth – the Harbor City of Lake Superior sends greetings to the "Zenith City"– connected by wire this day.

From the above dispatches the following answers were received:

- The "Metropolis of the New Wisconsin" hails with pleasure the completion of another link which binds the Harbor City to it in additional bonds of unity and friendship. Long may our family relations continue, and may the good God favor and bless all our efforts in developing the twin cities of northern Wisconsin.

- The citizen of Hudson cordially returns their greetings to the citizens of Bayfield and congratulates them upon the completion of the railway which shall tend to make our relations for the future closer than in the past. L. North- Mayor

- We congratulate you on this new link in the chain of Lake Superior cities. We rejoice in your growth and prosperity. – Mayor Duluth

- With pleasure I shake with you and all at Bayfield. – Henry M. Rice

- Superior City congratulates the Harbor City and rejoices with you and hopes your great expectation may now be speedily realized.

Noted further it is in the *Bayfield County Press* of October 20, 1883:

- Fred Fisher, a local merchant, "had the honor of being the first party to receive freight over the Omaha railway, receiving two carloads of lumber and supplies Wednesday. Frank Boutin is loading two cars with fish for shipment to points west over the *Omaha* road.

- The first regular passenger train to Bayfield will be put on Monday next for sure.

- Work on the railroad companies engine house progresses rapidly. The structures located on the corner of Fant Avenue and First Street at the end of the track.

- The Omaha pay car arrived in the village Thursday evening and made glad the hearts of 75 men of that company's employees paying them their monthly wages in shining gold.

- The railroad water tank is located at the foot of the ravine, just west of Pike's Mill.

- Tuesday the workmen engaged in excavating for the water main that is to supply the railroad tank in the ravine dug up the skeleton of what was once undoubtedly a fine specimen of the native red man of the woods. The skeleton with the exception of skull was reentered. The skull is unusually large, the jaws massive and supplied with a set of beautifully formed teeth, is now the property of Dr. Luce."

Bayfield Transfer's "Toonerville Trolley" In the Township of Russell: Circa 1900
Robert J. Nelson Collection

Bayfield Transfer—The Dalyrmple Gamble

Milwaukee Sentinel

Bayfield County Press - December 26, 1896

"Engineer Carrington has taken up his quarters in the Harbor City for a season. He is engaged in surveying for William F. Dalrymple" read the snippet in the October 20, 1883 *Bayfield County Press*. William Dalrymple held true to a vision to build a railroad line transporting grain from the Midwest to the east coast of the Union. In 1883 he founded the Bayfield Transfer Company with hopes to make his vision come true. Nearly thirteen years later the company, as the *Milwaukee Sentinel* reported, remained in a planing phase. By 1901 a few miles of track extended north toward Roy's Point and the Red Cliff Indian Reservation.

Misfortune then beholds the Dalrymple family. Included in the *Bayfield County Press*, July 27, 1901 reported it was that "Mr. William F. Dalrymple died at Pittsfield, Warren County Pennsylvania on July 21, 1901 after a severe illness of 15 days. Mr. Dalrymple was born in Sugar Grove, Warren County, April 17, 1825, and his boyhood days were spent there. As a young man he engaged in teaching school and was elected County school superintendent of Warren County. He afterwards engaged in oil and timber operations in Pennsylvania and later became one of the pioneers among the large wheat farmers market of North Dakota. He became interested in the future of Milwaukee and Bayfield and was firm in his belief that east lake ports would eventually become important cities, and as was characteristic, followed his belief with his investments and labors. The funeral was held July 24, 1901."

Yet the Bayfield Transfer Company persevered, resumed its business and transfer course operations and then was bought up by Wachsmuth Lumber Company in 1914. The "little train that could" ran its last run in the tall timbers of the Town of Russell in 1924 and the thoughts of extending the line beyond Racket Creek, Russell Township to Iron River and on to Duluth was dismissed.

The Press headlines this day in 1896 stated, *"We need 1 Million, Dalrymple Railway scheme at Bayfield. Seven miles of Transfer Line along the Lakefront of that City well underway, including the building of 100 peers – Mr. Dalrymple stops at the Pfister on his way east".*

W. F. Dalrymple of Bayfield, Wisconsin brother of Oliver Dalrymple, the Dakota farm king, was at the Milwaukee Pfister Hotel this morning in the interest of his railway holdings in northern Wisconsin. Mr. Dalrymple has been engaged for two years in building what is to be known as the Bayfield Transfer Railway, which extends along the lakefront of that total distance of 7 miles. The project includes the building of 100 solid peers on the lakefront, three of which are finished. The necessary grading is now about complete. The purpose of this transfer, 40 miles more of which is necessary, is to make Bayfield the terminus of the transcontinental lines, thus taking from Duluth a great deal of its immensely shipping traffic.

Before this additional 40 miles of road the County of Bayfield has voted bonds to the amount of $240,000. It will cost $1 million to put the road through to Iron River, from which point Bayfield is expected to draw business from the South Shore and Northern Pacific roads.

Mr. Dalrymple, who is president of the Bayfield Transfer Company, says the finest harbor on Lake Superior is at Bayfield. There is a depth of 100 feet of water and no dredging is necessary, as at Duluth. The people of Wisconsin, he says are more interested in the upbuilding of Bayfield than they are of Duluth, and will understand the great importance of the work he is carrying on.

Drawings which he has with him show an immense undertaking. He said he has expended a great deal of money so far, and had given the bigger amount for some men at work the past year, notwithstanding the stress of the times. In anticipation of the growth of Bayfield on account of the improvements being carried on much of the country in back the town has been plotted into lots. The road, which is to stem from Bayfield to Iron River, will also open a valuable pine and hardwood lands.

Mr. Dalrymple's visit to the Eastern states is for the purpose of interesting the Eastern capitalist in the proposed extension to Iron River in order to raise the balance of the some requested to complete it.

Bayfield Transfer Tracks South to Bayfield - North to Roy's Point
Burt Hill Photo – Pamela Hill-Barningham Collection

Chapter Seven
Two Lake Superior Experiences

The *Manistee*
Lake Superior South Shore Line Transit Company
BHA Pike Research Center Archive Collection

From the *Bayfield County Press* columns of November 24, 1883 it was stated, "all doubts of the fact that the propeller *Manistee* went down in the storm of last week have vanished and hope that was indulged in by uncertainty has given place to the set certainty that the popular boat and her genial officers have embarked for the sealess shores of eternity."

The sinking occurred east of the Michigan Island Lighthouse as Captain John McKay registered on a note, in a bottle that drifted to the beach near the Onion River that year. "'Just in sight of the Michigan Island Lighthouse- left Bayfield 11:10 PM—we may not survive this storm."

"Superior it is said never gives up her dead." Gordon Lightfoot

Samuel Stewart Vaughn
BHA Pike Research Center Archive Collection

The *Minnie V.* Visits the Garden of Eden

By Editor- Hank O. Fifield

Bayfield Press - December 12, 1870

The *Minnie V.* was one of the very early little steamers that plied the Chequamegon Bay area. A statement of work done and miles run for the year 1870 along with framed dimensions was forwarded to the editor by Engineer Patrick, an employee of Sam Vaughn. Before the voyage to Eden is propelled, and since a photo is not available, the following facts present additional insight about the time period this little tug. Mr. Patrick remits, "Enclosed find the statement of work done, number of trips made and miles run by the little steam yacht *Minnie V* of Bayfield for 1870: Total trips and miles, 305 trips and 5000 miles; Towed 4500 cords of logs in different rafts; Five scow loads of wood hay and shingle bolts; Towed three different vessels out of the harbor; and taken a large number of scow loads of lumber, etc., to the islands. The *Minnie V* was built at Blackrock, New York, New York in 1869, is 38 feet in length, 7 feet in breath and 3 feet deep in the hold. The *Minnie V* has one high-pressure boiler 6 feet long, 32 inches in diameter; one high-pressure engine, 7 inch diameter cylinder, with a 6 inch stroke. She has a stanchion deck, with seats fore and aft of the engine and can comfortably seat 45 passengers. She was purchased in Blackrock, in June 1869 by S. S. Vaughn, of this place, and steamed from there to Bayfield, being the smallest craft that ever passed through the Sault Ste. Marie. She now lies at anchor on the south side, having performed over the summers work without accident. No fears are had being driven from her mooring by Northeasters.

Ports of call include the following sites; Madeline Island north end with 16 stops, Oak Island Chapman and Company 8 stops; Sand Island 2 stops; Red Cliff 20 stops; Ashland 10 stops; Ashland West side 6 stops; Pikes Bay 12 stops; Michigan Island Lighthouse 2 stops; Bad River 10; Raspberry Island Lighthouse 1; Bass Island stone quarry 15; Presque Isle island 6; pleasure trip to Eastern excursion 5; Sand River 4; LaPointe 20; Sioux River 10; Siskowit Bay at Cornucopia 1; Outer Island 1; Wood yards Basswood Island 40; McClelland 12; Onion River 25; Buffalo Bay 20; Pleasure trips to Ashland bay and numerous other places of which no account has been, say 50. *Bayfield Press*, December 12, 1870. The wheel of the *Minnie V.* makes 8,400 revolutions an hour, and she runs about 8 miles in 60 minutes. August 5, 1871 *Bayfield Press*

Now on to a delightful trip to visit Vaughn's good friends at the Bad River Nation of Chippewa at Odanah, Wisconsin aboard the *Minnie V.*

Through the kindness of honorable S. S. Vaughn we took a trip to Odanah, the fair Indian village at the forks of the White and Bad Rivers. The course was taken to reach the reservation by way of the Kakagon River, and the tug *Minnie V* was soon steamed up and on her journey. Mr. Vaughn should be called Captain Cook number two, as he is a superior navigator. The Kakagon was never traversed by steam craft before this trip and the Captain was somewhat doubtful whether he could go to the "Gardens" with the tug, but was determined to give it a fair trial. We entered the river without experiencing any trouble, there being six to eight feet of water on the sandbar. After passing this point we struck deeper water and upstream for two miles it would average from one to two fathoms in the channel.

After entering the woodland area the river became more difficult to navigate, owing to its crooked course, but at full speed the noble tug made its way until we were within a mile of the "portage" when a few sunken logs caused a slight stoppage, which was soon passed and again we sped along at a rapid rate, at last reaching the crossing in safety, where all hands congratulated the Captain for his successful undertaking. The distance from Bayfield – twenty miles – was made in two hours and three quarters.

Considerable excitement among the natives was occasioned by the appearance of the tug from this direction, as they never had witnessed the like before, and large crowds came to the landing to welcome its arrival. We found the place in a flourishing condition and noticed several buildings had recently been erected, new fences built and a marked change in its appearance since our visit there last spring. The location of Odanah is really beautiful and contains a number of good buildings – one of which – the mission house – cost not less than $5000. It is now occupied by Reverend J. S. Mills who has charge of the missionary work in that vicinity. There are two neat churches, Presbyterian and Catholic, a good schoolhouse, three stores and a blacksmith shop, and contains some two or 300 inhabitants.

Through the hospitality of Mr. Walker (1), the government farmer, and his estimable lady, we partook of a bountiful repast, after which, we strolled about to see the fine gardens. Mr. Walker informs us that the Chippewa have raised 2500 bushels of potatoes, a large quantity of cabbages and other vegetables, and picked some 700 bushels of cranberries the season. The furred trade this year amounts to $6000 which is considered below the average sales. The government farmer harvested a fair crop of oats and wheat; corn is a tolerable good yield, while potatoes and other vegetables are most prolific. The hay crop is quite extensive and hundreds of tons have been secured. Mr. Walker thinks it is a good farming country.

Major Clark is having a large barn erected and workmen are now busy framing it. We noticed one improvement which is of great benefit and convenience to the Indians and that is, the "drawbridge" across Bad River. It is made of poles about the size of ordinary broomsticks, is in two sections, between which is a passageway for Mackinaw sailing boats and canoes. Each section floats on the water, having a boardwalk three feet wide with a substantial railing. One of the wings is arranged so as to swing open sufficiently to admit the passage of tugs and larger boats when required. It was wholly constructed by the Indian people with Joe Green as architect, and is a "big thing."

It is evident from the expressions of the Indians that they are much pleased with Major Clark's administration, which is thus far a successful one. Quite a large number of the noble Chippewa are congregated there, as the annual payment calls them from every direction, and this place is alive with their bright faces. As it was getting late the Captain thought it best to start and try and make the bay before dark. All aboard, the tug was soon underway and we reached the father of the lakes in time to enjoy a gentle Northeast sea as we passed the South channel, but arrived safely at the dock, well pleased with our short visit among Ye natives at the "Garden of Eden" of the Lake Superior region.

(1) Here we note that Major Clark provided similar services to the Red Cliff Band of Lake Superior Chippewa:

"A friend calls our attention to the following editorial notice of this place and our neighbor Major Clark. "Near Bayfield, a thrifty, charming village of 500 people, with substantial resources in his fisheries, brownstone quarries and lumber interests, is one of the Chippewa reservations, now in charge of Major S. A. Clark, formerly the assistant treasurer of the American Missionary Association at Chicago. The people are allowed in praise of the revolution that his coming has wrought. Like all the Indian agencies under the old system, it had been a nest of unclean things, rotten through and through Erie it but no little man has larger pluck and the major, and he took hold with a will at reform. Not only have his 5000 Chippewa received intact their annuities from the government, and then to a great degree protected from the leeches that fasten on the outskirts of every reservation, but he has had the signal success in persuading them to go to work.

He runs a large farm and the steam sawmill allowing them to work on their own book, and paying fair wages in money or in kind, and the Indians, as all Bayfield but the saloon keepers agree, have never been so prosperous before. It does not need many such experiments to justify the wisdom of our present Indian policy. Hereto for we have either babied or brutalized the red man. It is time to treat them like other men and women, guarding their individual rights, and holding them to individual good behavior". August 26, 1871 –Hank O. Fifield, Editor, *Bayfield Press*

The N. Boutin
Circa 1890s

James and Marge Miller Family Collection

Tales of the *N. Boutin*

Bayfield County Press - November 29, 1884

Commercial fisherman Nelson Boutin's steam tug at the *Boutin-Mahan* dock site is shown above located then near where the present day ferry boats land on the Harbor City's Front Street and Washington Avenue beachhead. The perils of operating a tug, iron clad or not lie the *Boutin* was , came into play daily in the lives of the old-time tugboat men. The *N Boutin*, by all standards surrendered to as superior by the olden wood planked vessels, was a workhorse. In addition to commercial fishing activities the Boutin, tugged rafted logs, pulled a grounded vessel to Bayfield dry docks and was the toughest of the tough. However, a hurricane or tornado the *N Boutin* was not, and, as the following story will dispatch, this steam tug did have limits.

The tug *N. Boutin*, owned by Messrs. Nelson Boutin and Sam Mahan, of Bayfield, left here Monday afternoon with 260 packages of fish for Ashland. When within about 2 miles of the central railway dock she encountered a large field of ice, but passed through it without much trouble. Shortly after passing this field and within several hundred feet of the dock she encountered the shore ice, fully 3 inches thick and tough as whalebone. By dint of persistent bucking they succeeded in reaching the dock and unloaded the cargo.

Probably had they then made about and steamed home all would have been well, but the tug *Fish* having brought over a pile driver, and being unable on account of the ice to get where her owners wanted it, the *Boutin* was pressed into the service and broke a channel for some distance through ice from 4 to 5 inches thick. Thereafter she started for Bayfield apparently all right. Out about and 2 miles from Washburn the firemen reported water in the fire hold. Engineer Thompson immediately investigated, not thinking, however that the boat was leaking. But his investigations were speedily cut short by the rapid increase of water and he reported to Mr. Boutin, the owner, that the boat was leaking badly and the chances for reaching shore decidedly slim. Help signals were sounded but failed to meet with response, the boat was headed directly for Washburn, throttle wide open.

All this happened in a very few minutes and they were fully two miles from Washburn when the water had risen to sufficient height to extinguish the fire in the boiler. When the fire was out they had just ninety pounds of steam and when she was beached, just east of the docket Washburn they had about forty pounds. Her bow struck bottom in seven feet of water, and the crew, six men all told, had scarcely reached shore when her stern settled in twelve feet and she careened over on the port side.

Wednesday night following, the tug *Favorite* with two lighters, went to Washburn and raised the sunken boat. On her starboard side, near the bow, one of her large iron plates had been torn off and a hole "3 x 16" was through her solid three-inch oak planking. The supposition is that bucking the ice to get to the pile driver an entire plate was torn off and the hole made. A mile further out in all probability lives would've been lost. Thursday morning the *Boutin* was brought to the port, the hole in her bow has been temporarily repaired and she is back engaged in steaming in and about the islands picking up fish, apparently none the worse for her encounter with Ashland ice. The *N. Boutin* is only three years old and is considered one of the very best tugs for her class on the lake, and has probably bucked more ice than any other tug on the lake during the past two years, and this is the first time she has ever come out second best.

Some years pass and at the time of the following story Bayfield Fish Company and Nelson Boutin, still owner and operator of the N. Boutin, were fishing out of the Port of Ontonogon, Michigan. The N. Boutin was then working as a company supply boat that often towed up to as many as nine small Mackinaw sailing boats astern with food and supplies to fishermen camped along the shorelines from ice-out in Bayfield late April to November election time. This company's commercial fishing operations ranged from shoreline points east of Ontonogon, Michigan, westward to Bark Point, Wisconsin and North to Isle Royale, Michigan. Here is a lighter duty and a fun side of life of the peoples suggested by this journey on the great waters. Editor Currie G. Bell shared in his paper a wonderful tale in an article entitled, *A Flying Trip to Boutinville* in the *Bayfield County Press* - June 18, 1887.

"The genial Captain Martin O'Malley of the tug *N. Boutin* gave the *Ontonogon Herald* scribe an invitation to accompany him on a trip to Bayfield on Saturday night last, and as the boat was to leave here at nine o'clock in the evening and return on Monday morning at six o'clock, we saw an opportunity of visiting a town which we had never before had seen, without at all interfering with our business, so we decided in a very few minutes to take it in.

Promptly at 8:45 o'clock we rounded the Ontonogon, Michigan pier and the tug, which is one of the fleetest on the lakes, shot out into Lake Superior and headed for Bayfield. The night was clear and the lake surface was as placid as a millpond. Seated in the pilot house we listened to numerous exploits related by the gallant captain, who by the way is a very good storyteller. We ran along very smoothly for some time, and although the *Boutin* was running at the rate of 11 or 12 miles an hour, not a shiver of her timbers was perceptible. About 35 miles from here we encountered a field of floating ice, through which we had to run under check. A slight fog towards break of day also impeded our progress, but promptly at five o'clock the staunch tug steamed into the Harbor City.

Bayfield is really a nice little city, but why they did not name it Boutinville is more than we can understand, for the first man we met was a Boutin and the last man we saw leaving was of the same name. The beautiful harbor and the orderly and neat appearance of the streets are that towns chief attractions. Taking a stroll uptown we soon came in sight of the courthouse and jail, which is built of stone and is a durable structure. The large well-kept building stands up on the hill overlooking the town schoolhouse. Bayfield Central (1) is a fine building and a credit to Bayfield.

Bayfield Central School Circa 1890
Robert J. Nelson Collection

A stone foundation and a pile of new lumber mark the spot where the new Island View Hotel is being erected. It will be a beauty and it is thought will greatly increase the summer travel to that place. As our time is limited we cannot go into detail in regard to the town.

The chief business seems to be fishing and lumbering. The buildings are well-kept and a resident met told us that the inhabitants are all well-to-do and contented. The local option liquor law which makes the license $500 is in effect there and has reduced the number of saloons so now there are but three in that place. Mr. Duffy Boutin runs one of them and has just recently put in bar fixtures that will cost them over $1000. Taken altogether, the Harbor City is one the finest resort towns on Lake Superior.

At five o'clock in the evening we boarded the *S. B. Barker* (2) and returned to Bayfield, nothing of interest occurring on the trip. After indulging in a good meal at the Lakeview Hotel we once more started out to take in the sights of the town. The first thing we did was to seek out brother Bell, of the *Bayfield County Press*, who we found to be a whole-soul gentlemen, doing a good business and having a neat, comfortable establishment. He has great faith in the Harbor City and has done as much as any of its citizens to help build up the town.

Shortly after leaving Bayfield, at 10 o'clock that night, we turned in and knew nothing of what occurred on the way down, until the *Boutin's* whistle blew upon entering Ontonogon at five o'clock next morning and awoke us. Altogether the trip was a very pleasant one which we shall not forget in some time. The crew of the *Boutin* is as follows: Captain- M. O'Malley; Engineer- N. Morrison; C. Schneider, and last but not least, Frank Smart, who attended to the culinary department. To each and every one of these gentleman's we present our thanks for numerous courtesies shown us on the trip."

(1)Bayfield Central was also referred to as the "Low School" and was located on four lots, 10 South 6th Street.

(2)The *Barker* was then a touring boat owned by the Wisconsin Central Railroad that transported passengers and goods around the Apostle Islands and Chequamegon Bay area into Ashland whereby the traveler could depart for anywhere in the world.

Commercial Fishermen in the Mackinaw
BHA Pike Research Center Archive Collection
1980-3-034

Perilous Waters

Bayfield County Press - August 28, 1880

To say that the name of Boutin and the Ed Boutin family especially, is synonymous with commercial fishing and bravery in Bayfield would be an understatement. In October of 1870 the established fishing and retail store firm of brothers Nelson and Frank Boutin and brothers, Joseph C., Duffy, Solomon, Felix, and Ed Boutin Sr. formerly of Laconia, Canada and Two Rivers, Wisconsin caste their fate to the wind and located their families and entire fishing operations to the Harbor City. The short story that follows reveals the bravery and character reflective of the Boutin family and pioneers fishermen of those days. This high seas battle tells of the heroics of Ed Boutin Sr.

A heavy nor'easter prevailed here from 11 o'clock Monday night until about six o'clock Wednesday evening. During all that time seas were running high and the wind blowing at a steady gale. The steamer *Pacific* laid here nearly all day Tuesday, which was obliged to put back to Duluth after being tossed on the waves all night on Monday, arrived here at five o'clock Wednesday morning. She soon left for the outside, but was compelled to seek shelter near the leeward shore of Presque Isle until nearly dark Wednesday night.

Wednesday afternoon, three Mackinaw fishing boats belonging in Bayfield, started from Ontonagon, Michigan for this place. The boats contained Ed Boutin, John Le Coy and an Ontonagon fisherman in the first, Johnny Richards of Bayfield and Joe Allie of Houghton, in the second, and Fred Breager and Charles Gilbault in the third. While sailing in the above order about 18 miles outside and east of Michigan Island at four o'clock, Richards's boat capsized.

Those in the leading boat noticed the accident after time, but as a third boat was behind, they merely lay by, expecting to see the men picked up. But instead the last boat kept on her course and passed the men that were clinging for life to the overturned boat.

Ed Boutin accordingly began to beat back to the capsized sail in the heavy sea, and succeeded in making the rescue at the risk of being capsized himself. The other boat did not even lie by to see whether Boutin was successful in his attempt to save the man or whether he ensured their fate. Richard's boat and all in it was lost. This is the only one of many times that Ed Boutin has come through terrible experiences of wind and wave on this lake and it is not the first time he saved his fellow fishermen from drowning. We trust that he who is brave and fearless enough to cheat old Superior of her victims at the risk of his own life will continue well to weather every storm that may overtake him, afloat or ashore.

Apostle Islands, Wis. Lake Superior. Michigan Island Light House.

Michigan Island Lighthouse
BHA Pike Research Center Archive Collection

Alice Craig Facsimile
Author's pencil sketch

Tales of The Little Schooner *Alice Craig*

By Robert J. Nelson

The schooner *Alice Craig* appeared similar to the above cut of the "Revenue Cutter" *Massachusetts*; a small and sometimes lightly armed gun boat used by the Federal government in the 1800s to enforce customs and regulations. The *Craig*, also built as a Revenue Cutter, aka Alice Krieg, found her destiny with the Frank and Nelson Boutin commercial fishing family of Bayfield, Wisconsin. The company flagship, she would ply the waters from Bayfield along the south shore of Wisconsin from Duluth, Minnesota to Isle Royale and near Marquette Michigan.

As the *Craig* sailed the shores Lake Michigan and Eastern Lake Superior toward her new home port in Bayfield, she carried a valuable cargo of Boutin family members and fishermen. On her spacious decks were twelve pound nets, 650 gill nets and enough equipment needed to start a fishing enterprise. Mackinaws, usually 26 foot sail rigs were towed astern, or if fair winds prevailed to the advantage of the skipper fishermen, the Mackinaws were freed and left to sail independently. The contingency of former French Canadians arrived to Bayfield from Two Rivers, Wisconsin in August of 1870.

Here follows a series of chronological news releases from excerpts related to the *Craig's* Lake Superior commercial fishing trade, her captain's exploits, the final tragedy and resting spot in Davy Jones locker.

December 9, 1871: The schooner *Alice* Craig of this place left for Duluth two weeks ago Thursday, and arrived within six days in reaching the Zenith City, owing to headwinds. She left Duluth on Saturday, December 2, at 10:00 AM for this port, having an assorted cargo for our merchants and let off at Steamboat Island when the wind suddenly shifted to Northeast – with heavy seas, which passed clear over the staunch little craft. Captain Nelson Boutin had seen it was impossible to make Sand Island, turned around and made for Bark Point bay, about 45 miles from Bayfield, where she is now frozen in the ice.

It was midnight when the storm struck her and very dark and cold; the wind blew a perfect gale, tearing away her jibs and carrying her foresail considerably. We learn the rigging was broken. The same seas caused the yawl boat to break its fastening, but it was saved. Her hold and rigging was covered with ice, and the ropes frozen stiff. The Captain was ably assisted by his crew and passengers. Our genial landlord, Captain Phillip W. Smith who by the way was once a sailor, rendered valuable service to Captain Boutin and Major Sam Mahan. A Mr. Clark was a passenger, and stood the storm mentally. On Sunday morning, Captain Boutin finding the vessel frozen in solidly, decided to leave her for the winter. An Indian was sent here with letters which gave our people the first knowledge of the vessel's whereabouts. Teams and packers were sent out to meet the party were found near Moose Lake, having left Bark Point on Tuesday morning. They arrived home Thursday night, being tired and foot sore from the trip. We understand that a few men left here Thursday morning by water, for Bark Point, in hopes of getting the vessel afloat, what with what success we have not yet learned. *Bayfield Press* (the preparer notes that no further story or information there-in compliments this tale; the Craig was floated as she lived to serve another day.)

November 27, 1880 – Saturday: Last Saturday night, November 20, Nelson and Frank Boutin's staunch little fishing Schooner, the *Alice Craig* under Captain Murphy, sailed from Duluth with over 50 tons of flour, feed, pork, oil, and general merchandise. A telegram was received here, announcing her sailing with a frozen center board. The next heard from her was from Joe Boutin and Michael Coucher, two of her crew, who arrived here in the small boat Monday afternoon, with news that the vessel was ashore on the Northeast side of Wilson's island. Michael's feet were badly frozen when he got here.

The *Craig* was struck by a heavy sea early Sunday morning. Having no use of the center board, the wheel being frozen, and the chains frozen so anchors could not be dropped, she was at the mercy of the waves, which threw her upon the beach at five o'clock Sunday morning.

Six men, John Gonyon, Ed Boutin Sr., Ed Boutin Jr., John Drouillard, Mike Drago, and one other, started for the vessel the same afternoon, to remove enough of her cargo to the island so she could be floated from the shore. They also took out fuel.

Tuesday morning the tug *T. H. Camp* under Captain Harris started for the vessel through the ice that had covered the harbor the night before. The *Craig* looking more like an iceberg than anything else was afloat before the tug reached her. Freight was put back on board, and in the tow of the *Camp* she started for Bayfield in a snowstorm, with more ice rapidly forming. Open water along the west side of Madeline Island was followed until they reached a point opposite of Bayfield, when they had to push through several miles of ice about 2 inches thick.

The *Camp* with light sheathing, and that was gone off one side, had to stop several times to make steam. The passage was made all the more difficult by the helplessness of the *Craig* which, her rudder being useless and frozen to one side, would not tow directly aft of the tug. The dim outlines of the vessels were distinguished through the storm about four o'clock in the afternoon, but not until after six did the shouts from the dock and vessel announce that the plucky little *Camp* had won, and the *Alice Craig* was safe with all her cargo. Aside from her broken wheel the vessel is not injured. The tug *Camp* received $75 for the job, worth at least $500 to Nelson and Frank Boutin, the owners. *Bayfield Press*

Fall 1882: the work of repairing Frank Boutin's Schooner *Alice Craig*, which went ashore unmanned during the heavy gale last fall, was inaugurated this week and will be pushed rapidly. *Bayfield County Press*, April 21, 1883

April 28, 1883: the schooner *Alice Craig* was in place upon the dry dock this week, and the work of repairing the damage she sustained last fall progresses finely. *Bayfield County Press*, April 28, 1883.

November 26, 1887: *Frank Boutin's schooner, the "Alice Craig", is no more.* She left this port Friday with a cargo of supplies for his camp at Siskiwit/*Cornucopia, Wisconsin,* was caught in the gale of that night and went ashore near Bark Point. Her crew of five men succeeded in reaching shore in the morning and walked through the woods to Bayfield. The *Craig* was built and used as a revenue cutter for several years and was purchased by Mr. Boutin at Chicago in 1867, and brought to this point to be used in the fishing business in 1867. At that time she was considered the fastest and handsomest fishing craft on the lake. In 1877 she was wrecked at Duluth, afterwards raised, and fitted up as a pleasure yacht by Duluth parties, but this not proving profitable she was repurchased by Mr. Boutin and been used in the fishing business exclusively since. Captain Bunker who sailed her from Chicago here, has commanded her almost every season since 1867, and was in command of her last voyage. He is now quite ill from the effects of the exposure. Mr. Boutins loss will run into the thousands. *Bayfield County Press*

November 21, 1887: the schooner *Alice Craig*, of Bayfield, Wisconsin, owned and operated by Nelson and Frank Boutin, a class B vessel, 42 tons, home port of Bayfield, Wisconsin, went ashore near Bayfield, Lake Superior, and became a total property loss, hull $2,500 cargo $2,000 – 1887 Casualty List (Total loss)--*Marine Record*, Dec. 15, 1887

Further from the *Port Huron Daily Times*; Friday, November 25, 1887, the *Times* state that, "the Schooner Alice Craig went ashore, Monday night near Bayfield. *The Marine Record*, Thursday, November 24, 1887 p.1, affirms the sinking.

"Ashland—-Monday night the schooner *Alice Craig*, laden with camp supplies, was driven ashore near Bayfield and went to pieces. The crew escaped in a yawl and landed in a dense forest. A blinding snow storm was raging, and the crew got lost. After wandering about in the woods for hours, with their clothing covered with ice and almost perishing from cold and hunger, the crew, with the exception of Captain Bunker, reached Bayfield and reported that the captain had laid down in the snow to die, having become so exhausted that he could not walk. The others were so worn out that they could not help him. A rescuing party was at once organized, and after a long search they found the Captain. He was insensible and his limbs were badly frozen; he was brought here, and there are but little hopes of his recovery. The vessel was owned by N. Boutin, of Bayfield.

The *T. H. Camp* at Booth Fisheries Dock
RJN.BH.1899.007

Booth's Tug *T. H. Camp* Sleeps in 30 Fathom

Bayfield County Press

Saturday, November 24, 1900

The T. H. Camp goes down in 30 fathoms with a load of supplies; the crew rescued by a sailboat that was near when the tug started to go down read the headlines of the Press this date.

The tug *T. H. Camp,* one of A. Booth and Company's fishing tugs went down last Friday afternoon in the middle of the channel between Bass and Madeleine Islands. *The Camp* left Ashland shortly after one o'clock with a load of camp supplies for W. T. Gardner and Company's lumber camp at the head of Madeline Island. When nearly opposite the stone quarry on Bass Island the tug stopped to pick up Frank Shaw, Junior, who was out there in a sailboat, calculating to take him in tow and use his boat to unload supplies at the island.

As the tug slowed up she listed badly, causing the cargo to shift and soon the hold began to fill with water. About this time the sailboat came alongside and took the crew off the sinking boat. They have hardly got aboard the sailboat when the tug settled and went down stern first in

30 fathoms of water. Had the sail boat not been there to take the crew off it is very probable that some, if not all, of the crew would have drowned, for they would have been precipitated into the water as soon as the boat went under. The yawl boat floated on the surface but it is doubtful if any of the crew would have been able to get to it before they were chilled through by the icy water. The sailboat brought the crew to shore and the accident was reported to the company.

The crew consisted of Captain John Swanes; George McNeill, engineer and Gus Maebius, firemen. Daniel Cronk, of Ashland, engineer on the *Plowboy*, was aboard and was the only one to get into the water. As he attempted to jump into the sailboat he fell into the water but managed to grasp a line on the sailboat and was pulled in but not before he was up to his waist. George McNeill lost some clothes and a number of tools while the fireman was more unfortunate. He had all his clothes and personal effects aboard. His loss was about $300.

The *Camp* was built at Cape Vincent, New York and was valued at $4000 with no insurance. The loss to W. T. Gardner and Company is about $1000 and will be a severe blow to their logging operations.

Chapter Eight
A Chronological Time Line
11,000 BP to 1856

CHIPPEWA HOUSE.

Frank Leslie's Illustrated Newspaper

No. 1660 – Volume LXIY

New York, New York

For the week ending July 9, 1887

Robert J. Nelson Collection

The chronological orders of events relevant to the history of the New Wisconsin and Lake Superior region are excerpts from my personal notebook taken over the years. They represent the knowledge of a wide range of reputable scholars, author's and article contributors.

Information sources include; Boyce, W. D. *Industries of Bayfield*- October1883, St. Paul-The Pacific Publishing Co.; Burnham, Guy & Moses Strong, *Historical Sketches-The Lake Superior Country in History and Story*, Busch, Jane C. Ph.D., *People and Places: A Human History of the Apostle Islands*, which was prepared under contract to Midwest Regional Office, National Park Service-United States Department of the Interior-2008, Omaha-2008; Chapple John B., the *Wisconsin Islands- The Famous APOSTLE ISLANDS at the Top of Wisconsin*, Ashland Daily Press, Ashland, WI, 1945; Houkom, John A., Pastor Bethesda Lutheran Church, 1943; Knight, Eleanor, *Tales of Bayfield Pioneers- A History of Bayfield*, 2008; Ross, Hamilton Nelson, *La Pointe, Village Outpost*, 1960, North Central Printing, St. Paul, MN; Schafer, Joseph *Outline History of Wisconsin*; 1925 *Wisconsin Bluebook*; *History of Bayfield County- The History of Northern Wisconsin*, Western Historical Co. Chicago-1881; *The Bayfield Mercury, Bayfield Gazette, Bayfield Press, Bayfield County Press, Bayfield Progress* individually in the time frame 1857-1927

11,000 BP: Native American peoples were evidenced as present in the Chequamegon Region. The earliest indications of the Woodland Indian in the Apostle Island area are groups of peoples that date back 1200 years. The Woodland tradition appears in the region about 2,100 BP.

Pre-1435: The prospectors of the Minnesota Mining Company investigated an old and partially filled-in shaft c- 1848 which had evidently been sunk by the Indians (The Ontonogon District of the Gogebic Range). Prehistoric axes, hatchets, were found in the pit as well as a growing hemlock tree, which when cut, displayed growth rings indicating an age of 395 years.

1490: It was believed that the Ojibway left their former home on the Gulf of St. Lawrence and after trekking for several years arrived in the Chequamegon Point (Long Island) region, 1490. Their brethren, later called the Ottawa, took up home near Montreal.

1500: The Ojibway arrive at Chequamegon Point, also spelled frequently as Che-quam-ik, Che-gol-me-gon, Chequamic, Chewamic, Chegoiamegon, that is located on the western end of the present day Long Island.

1512-1627: Civil governance of the Chequamegon Bay area is under the flag of Spain.

1534: Jacques Cartier discovers the Gulf of St. Lawrence and in1535 he had explored as far as Montreal where further exploration was halted by the rapids. Cartier made another trip in 1641 but was halted by the Iroquois.

1557: "It is said that the Missionaries even visited Ste. Magdaline Island *(now Madeline)* as early as 1641; but there is nothing certain about it. Indian tradition says that ten generations or about 350 years ago, the Ojibway had their principal city upon this island. The old men of the tribe have even pointed out to the writer the location and they say that this was their "Holy City" the place where their "Sacred Fire" was ever kept burning. But there came a day when their fire was extinguished. Then, with tears in their eyes, they will tell you there is no escape, the penalty, according to the tradition, was even so.

The Ojibway Indians called the settlement at LaPointe, Shay-ok-wam-ik-ong, meaning "the place at long, sandy point." The long sandy island directly opposite the site of the old settlement was once a peninsula, extending out from the mainland, and on that account was called and is still known as "Shak-oh-wam-ik" The French writers in speaking of the old settlement after it became a trading post always used the Indian name and spelled it thus: Che-gol-me-gon, which is a very close imitation of the Ojibway pronunciation. The Ojibway name for Madeline Island is Mo-ning-wun-a-kan-ing, meaning "the place where yellow-hammers are to be found." Birds of various varieties, the yellow-hammer predominating, have frequented the island in the early spring time as far back as the memory of man runneth – hence the name."

1600 to perhaps 1620: The Chippewa remain in the Chequamegon mainland area and then took up abode at the "Soo."

1607-1776: The Wisconsin area is claimed under the Virginia Charter as part of the Colony of Virginia.

1618: Before the Pilgrims arrived at Plymouth in the Mayflower, Samuel de Champlain, who founded Quebec in 1608, discovered Madeline Island in 1618. Champlain and his associates were the first white men who saw the Chippewa peoples

1622-23: Etienne Brule skirted the shore of Lake Superior & "accepted as fact that he was the first white man of record to see Lake Superior in 1622. The diary of Grenolle who accompanied Brule, noted the that Ojibway were calling the rapids of the present Sault St. Marie, the Sault de Gaston, named after Louis XIII brother, indicating white men of French descent were prior visitors.

1627-1762: Civil governance of the Chequamegon Bay area is under the flag of France.

1632: Samuel de Champlain publishes the first map of "The Father of All Lakes."

1634: Jean Nicolet is the first white man to view Lake Superior, but ventures no further West, but instead directs his course to the Green Bay & Mississippi River area.

1641: Jesuits Charles Raymbault & Isaac Jogues arrive at Sault de Sainte Marie and give name: "The Rapids of St. Mary." It was at this time Lake Superior was called Grand Lac du Nadouessioiu. The Nadowe are mentioned here as living 18 days West (9 days by canoe and then 9 days from either the Brule or St. Louis River to the Iroquois site) of the St. Mary's River.

1648: Being persecuted by the Iroquois the Huron and Ottawa arrive at Chequamegon. The Sac and Foxes arrive similarly. Both tribes remain in the Chequamegon area until 1671 with the return of the Chippewa.

1659: First Jesuit Church is constructed at La Pointe.

1659 and spring 1660: Pierre Esprit Radisson and his brother-in-law, trapper Sueur des Groseillier and trapper Medart Chouart, with six other fur traders and a band of Huron and Ottawa Indians, skirted the south shore of Lake Superior, learned of mines of copper in the neighborhood, and late in the autumn entered Chequamegon Bay. Somewhere between the Ashland and Washburn of our day, they built a crude waterside fort. Later caching their stores, to hide them from the Indians, they visited a Huron village in the interior and wandered as far west as the Mille Lacs region in Minnesota, there wintering among the Ojibway. In the spring they visited the Sioux and then returned to Chequamegon Bay, built another fortified trading post, and during the following summer descended to Canada, never again to visit the Northwest.

This account states that Radisson and Groseillier arrive near mouths of Fish and Whittlesey creeks, West of Ashland.

1660: The first missionary who landed at La Pointe was Reverend Father Menard, who was said to have been murdered this year by the Algonquian Indians on the rapids of the Menomonie River. "He was sent to Wisconsin in the winter of 1660-1661 to regenerate the Ottawa, a band that roamed in the forest near the southern shore of Lake Superior. The reception accorded this old man, then aged 55, by his charges was far from encouraging. Sunk to the lowest depths of savage degradation, they mocked at his teaching, enacted obscene celebrations before his eyes, and at length drove him from their cabins. He was forced in the heath of winter to seek shelter in a rude hut constructed from fir boughs. Compelled to subsist for the most part on vile refuse, acorns, bark and moss, he very nearly died of starvation.

1661: Father Rene Menard: Is first missionary to Wisconsin Indians.

1665: October 1: Father Claude Allouez, first white-man, reached the Chequamegon Bay. It is believed that for a short time Father Allouez was located at the place now known as Pike's Bay, the precise spot not being known. One tradition designates Section 22 another Section 27 Township 50 N., Range 4-3 W (Sections 22 & 27 intersect at a point approximately 300' North of Pikes Creek). Two other Jesuit missionaries arrive to perfect the work of Allouez, Jacque Marquette and Louis Nicholas.

4000 Indian people live in Chequamegon area that included the Huron and Ottawa branches so- named the Osakis or Sauk; the Outagamie or Fox, and the Illinois.

Father Allouez, the exploring priest, established a chapel on Chequamegon Bay in an Indian Village. The region of the mission was called, "La Pointe du Saint Esprit"-"The point of the holy spirit" & "when he first arrived there were two Indian villages; the first was Ottawa at Fish Creek with some 800 fighting men & 2000 persons with 40-50 large cabins- this includes several other tribes; Potawatomi, Illini, Sauk, Fox and Cree, and the second Huron bands who had settled near Bono's Creek. The location is presumed near Boyd's Creek.

1669: Father Marquette visited Father Allouez chapel and left from there to found a mission at Green Bay, WI. In 1669 Allouez was relieved by Father Jacques Marquette.

1670: Hudson Bay Company is formed when Groseillier finds interest with English merchants in a group named "Company of Adventurers."

1671: Between the departure of Father Marquette from the area in this year and the arrival of Le Sueur the Chippewa return to the Chequamegon area from the Sault Saint Marie area. Since this time Chequamegon has always been regarded as their ancestral home.

1673: Father Marquette's map assigns the name "Lac Superior De Tracy."

1678-80: Daniel Greysolon Duluth explored and traded in the western end of Lake Superior, discovering the Bois Brule St. Croix route to the Mississippi, and hunting with Sioux Indians on Wisconsin soil. By 1680 the Ojibwa had a village at Chequamegon, either on the mainland or at La Pointe.

1680: "Our neighboring Village of La Pointe on Madeline Island, should celebrate its second centennial on the 14th of next August. It was settled by the whites, August 14, 1680." *Bayfield Press*, May 1, 1880

1690: About this time the French built a trading post on the sand spit that was then known as La Pointe. In 1693 Pierre Le Sueur moved this trading post to a more defensible location on the Southern end of Madeline Island Grants Point, then known to the French as Isle Michel.

1692: A fort and trading post was erected near where the Catholic Indian burial ground is located, between the Village of LaPointe and the Old Mission Resort. Pierre Charles le Sucur, under instructions of Frontenac, Governor of New France (Canada) erected on the point near the site of the Mission, the first fort built on Lake Superior. The island was selected on account of the natural protection against sudden attacks of an enemy. For the same reasons, the Chippewa, Ottawa, and Huron Indians selected this site. Their homes and families were here and their fields of waving corn, tobacco, and potatoes were comparatively safe from the depredations of their enemies, the Sioux and the Foxes, who frequented the country from the south and west, even up to the opposite shore of the mainland. A feeling of security certainly was to be preferred. The earliest traders were transitory, continually changing their locations to suit the Indians. The forts, several of which were built on the Great Lakes for the protection of traders, were of little practical use; the natives nearly always living on the friendliest terms with the white traders.

French officers following Le Sueur; Captain Paul Legardneur St. Pierre- 1718; Ensign Linctot- 1720, the Great La Ronde- 1724, Marin- 1748, de Beaubassin (last officer-1758), and finally an officer named St. Luc.

1693: Continued wars between the Sioux and the Wisconsin tribes rendered the route through Wisconsin unsafe for French traders. Count Frontenac thereupon sent Pierre Charles le Sueur to command at Chequamegon and keep open a route from Lake Superior to the Mississippi. He built a stockade and fort at La Pointe, on Madeline Island in Chequamegon Bay, and another on an island in the Mississippi near Red Wing, Minnesota. At this time the French named Madeline Island St. Esprit, after the earlier calling of Chequamegon Bay and Allouez mission. Until the arrival of the English it was successively called Isle Detour, La Pointe, La Ronde, St. Michael's and Montreal.

1698: A summary of French Commanders at La Pointe: Pierre Le Sueur 1693-1698; Paul Le Gardier, Sueur de St. Pierre 1718-1720; Rene Godefroy, Sueur de Linctot 1720-1726; Louis Denis, Sueur de la Ronde 1727-1721: Phillipe Louis Denis de la Ronde 1741-1743; Madame La Ronde (wife of Louis) 1743-1748; Joseph Gaultier, Chevalier de la Verendrye 1751-1755; Pierre Hertel de Beaubassin 1756-1758; Sueur Corne de la St. Luc.

1718: Captain St. Pierre and Ensign Linctot construct the second French post at Chequamegon. This was located in Sandy Bay (Wikwedwangag) nearby to the Mission Inn landscape & known as Middle Fort.

This fort would be re-established at the new location on the West side of Madeline Island. This fort served the area for more than 40 years. As early as the Northwest Fur Company established a trading post at La Pointe the government of New France occupied the southeast point of the island with a fort garrisoned by a company of French regulars. This fort was built by a man named Captain St Perrie. The old fort exists on May 29, 1859 as Reverend James Peet arrives there to pick up garden plants.

1727: Madeline Island was known then as St. Michel. During this time period, the name Apostle Islands appeared on maps. La Ronde was assigned duty at Chequamegon: he was the first practical miner of copper and the first to introduce European style civilization to the region. He had a garrison at the fort at Madeline Island where he kept horses, a dock, probably a mill and attempted to farm.

1736: About the time of La Ronde, it was that the Chippewa obtained a footing west of Lake Superior and that the Chippewa became aggressive and began to drive the Sioux to the Great Plains.

1744: The name, Apostle Islands, probably given by the Jesuits, came into official use during this time period; it appears on a French map dated 1744.

1754-1760: The Ojibwa fight for the French during the French and Indian War. Following their defeat, the French abandoned the La Pointe trading post. The British destroyed this post in 1765.

1756: Hertel de Beaubassin was assigned to, and is the last French officer in command of the Chequamegon post. This was about the time Ojibway Chief, Waub-o-jeeg of Chequamegon, was fighting with the British.

1763-1783: Civil governance of the Chequamegon Bay area is under the Flag of Great Britain.

February 10, 1763: The Treaty of Paris 1763 is signed whereby the vast French territories came into the hands of the British. Fur trade in the Lake Superior region would not resume until 1765 when Alexander Henry, an English subject from New Jersey, secured a trading concession to the area. The Ojibway were in particular hostile to the British. They captured the fort at Mackinac this day and killed or abused the entire garrison. Staging a lacrosse game, the ball in an apparent accidental manner was thrown over the palisades, and then stormed after it through the open gates.

July 26, 1765: Having secured trading rights on Lake Superior for 3 years, Alexander Henry sets out for Chequamegon Bay. His cargo included four canoes (4.5 x 36'capable of carrying 4 and an 8 man crew), weighed 5 tons, and he hired French voyageurs at rate of one hundred pounds of beaver skins per year, per man plus the following which comprised of one bushel of corn and two pounds of fat per month per man.

Eastern Territorial Map 1775
BHA Pike Research Center Archive Collection

August: British fur trader Alexander Henry arrived at Chequamegon Bay to reopen fur trade on western Lake Superior. On the mainland near Chequamegon Bay, Henry found and Ojibwa village of seven to eight hundred people. Henry partnered with Jean Baptiste Cadotte (Cadeaux) of Sault Saint Marie.

Further, Alexander Henry, a trader, landed at what is now Bayfield and built a house just below Chapman & Company's store. *(Block 119)* He called the place Chagamawig and said he found 50 lodges of Indians living there. An "old-timer" in the *Bayfield County Press* of *April 15, 1904* states that he first cabin to be built here was in August 1765, not March 24 of 1856. It was built by Alexander Henry, a trader, just below where Mr. Chapman's store used to stand.

December 15, 1765: Alexander Henry reports "the bay is entirely frozen over." On April 20, 1766, the ice broke up, and several canoes arrived filled with women and children, who reported that the men of their land were all gone out to war against the Nadowessies, or Sioux.

1774: The *Quebec Act of 1774* makes Wisconsin a part of the Province of Quebec. This act of the Parliament of Great Britain set procedures for the governance of the Province of Quebec. The province's territory was expanded to take over part of the "Indian Reserve" and included much of what are now southern Ontario, Illinois, Indiana, Michigan, Ohio, and Wisconsin. It guaranteed practice of Catholicism, restored French civil law for private matters and maintained the use of English common law for public administration.

BHA Pike Research Center Archive Collection

1779: Fur traders, with the financial backing of Montreal Scotsmen (ancestral enemies of the English Hudson's Bay Company) formed the North West Company to better maintain themselves against the established industry giant. Alexander Henry remains as an independent trader who worked in harmony with acknowledged North West Company association heads, Benjamin and Joseph Frobisher and Simon McTavish.

1782: Michael Cadotte, Jean Baptiste Cadotte's younger son, arrived in the area as a factor for the Alexander Henry-Jean Baptiste Cadotte business relationship. He spent little or no time at La Pointe; the Middle Fort trading site was destroyed, but spent time in Lac Du Flambeau and Lac Courte Oreilles and traded at the head of the old Flambeau Trail at the Montreal River.

1783: Civil governance of the Chequamegon Bay area was facilitated through the Northwest Territory Act with the end of the Revolutionary War in 1783, the United States government acquiesced to Virginia. A group of traders and merchants decided to cooperate and entered into a formal partnership called the North West Company and began the domination of fur trade in the area.

1787-1800: Civil governance of the Chequamegon Bay area was facilitated through the Northwest Territory.

July 13, 1787: Ordinance of 1787, an Ordinance for the Government of the Territory of the United States, North-West of the River Ohio, and was also known as the Freedom Ordinance. The ordinance was an act of the Congress of the Confederation of the United States and was the first organized territory of the United States out of the region south of the Great Lakes, north and west of the Ohio River and east of the Mississippi River.

1791: John Johnston, born in Craige, Antrim County, Ireland in 1762, arrives to the La Pointe area that fall. While at La Pointe he married Shagowashcodawaqua, Women of the Green Glades, daughter of Waubojeeg, Chief White Fisher, in 1793 and moves to the Sault St. Marie area to raise four sons, four daughters. He died at the Sault St/ Marie in 1828.

In this period Michael Cadotte marries Equaysayway, Traveling Woman, and daughter of Chief White Crane- Waubijejauk. The chief's home was on the mainland near Bayfield. Married at the Sault Ste. Marie, Equaysayway was also christened as Madeline, to which the island is named.

1790 Old Northwest Territory
BHA Pike Research Center Archive Collection

1792: John Johnston built a fur-trade post on Chequamegon Bay. Jean Baptiste Cadotte, of the Chequamegon region, and the father of the famous Michael Cadotte, had married an Indian girl at the Sault Saint Marie. They had two sons; Jean Baptiste Cadotte and the other Michael Cadotte. Michael Cadotte came to Madeline Island to stay.

John Wilson, the "Hermit of Wilson Island" and that of buried treasure fame, was born in Canada of Scottish parentage. In October of 1846, after losing in a fight to Judge John "King" Bell at La Pointe, Wilson packed his canoe, paddled to the island and built a cabin in which he lived until his death by "delirium tremens" in 1869. He is buried at La Pointe's hillside cemetery.

1793: Michel Cadotte, son of Jean Baptiste Cadotte serves charge of the North West Company post at La Pointe. For the company's post, Cadotte chose a site on the south end of Madeline Island a short distance from the old fort built by Le Sueur in 1693.

1800-1809: Civil governance of the Chequamegon Bay area was facilitated through the Indiana Territory.

1808: John Jacob Astor organized American Fur Company, and received a charter from New York State to operate for 25 years. The North West Company & Mackinac Company partnered with John Jacob Astor's American Fur Company to form the South West Company.

1809-1818: Civil governance of the Chequamegon Bay area was facilitated through the Illinois Territory.

1810: John Jacob Astor purchased the Mackinac Company and organized the South West Fur Company.

1811: The Southwest Company, a partnership of Mackinac Company and North West Company and now Astor's American Fur Company, surfaced to avoid onerous American taxes.

1812- 1815: War of 1812: A military conflict was fought between the forces of the United States of America and those of the British Empire. The Americans declared war in 1812 for a number of reasons, including a desire for expansion into the Northwest Territory, trade restrictions because of Britain's ongoing war with France impressments of merchant sailors into the Royal Navy, British support of American Indian tribes against American expansion, and the humiliation of American honor. Until 1814, the British Empire adopted a defensive strategy, repelling multiple American invasions of the provinces of upper and Lower Canada.

1816: After the War of 1812, British forces took possession of the Chequamegon country at La Pointe. Michael Cadotte was then in possession of the old fort located on the SE corner of Madeline Island. American Fur Company is in sole possession of La Pointe trade, with Michel Cadotte as its factor.

1818-1836: Civil governance of the Chequamegon Bay area was facilitated through the Michigan Territory. Michigan divided the area of Wisconsin into three governing counties; Michilimackinac (1818-1826), Brown and Crawford. Chippewa County (1826-1838) split from Michilimackinac County with the County seat at Sault Saint Marie.

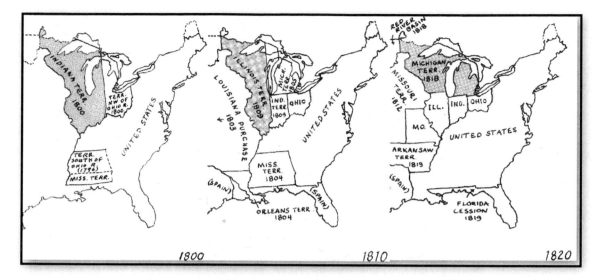

Indiana Territory 1800-1809, Illinois Territory 1809-1818,
Michigan Territory 1818-1836
BHA Pike Research Center Archive Collection

1818: October, the County of Michilimackinac, which included all of the present State of Wisconsin north of a line passing west from the head of De Noquet Bay, was created by Lewis Cass, then Governor of the Territory of Michigan. John Jacob Astor made La Pointe headquarters for the northwest trade of the American Fur Company.

Brothers, Lyman and Truman Warren began working the fur trade in the Chequamegon area for North West Company and within a couple of years switched to working for American Fur Company and married two of Michel Cadotte' s daughters and in 1823 Cadotte sold the Warrens his trading business. Truman Abraham & Lyman Marcus Warren, from New England, arrived as independent traders at Lac du Flambeau and Lac Courte Oreilles villages. Both men were recognized and hired by American Fur Company as competent traders and arrived to La Pointe circa 1820.

Warren marriages to Michel Cadotte daughters; Truman married Charlotte (aged 16)-Lyman married Marie (aged 21). In 1823 the Warrens purchase Michel Cadotte's interest in American Fur Company.

La Pointe was still located on the southern end of the Island, not yet being moved to its present site.

1820: The Lewis Cass Expedition of 1820 was a survey of the western part of Michigan Territory led by Lewis Cass, governor of the territory. On January 14, 1820, United States Secretary of War John C. Calhoun authorized the governor of Michigan Territory, Lewis Cass, to lead a party of scientists, soldiers, Canadian voyageurs, and Native Americans into the wilderness of western

Michigan Territory. The purpose of the expedition was to survey the geography and topography of the region in order to produce a complete map, survey the flora and fauna of the region, survey the Indians of the region, their numbers, tribes, customs, and loyalties, whether to the United States or Great Britain, select and purchase sites for forts, especially at Sault St. Marie, survey the geology of the region, especially with regard to commercially valuable minerals and search for the source of the Mississippi River.

The Cass-Schoolcraft party visit La Pointe. The point of land now known as and Long Island was called Chequamegon Point, while the bay itself was called "The Bay of St. Charles."

1821: Chequamegon Point is separated thus forming the present Long Island.

1823-25: British Admiral Henry Wolsey Bayfield surveys and maps the Chequamegon Bay area. Bayfield is thereafter so-named by Henry M. Rice in Bayfield's honor.

1825: *The Treaty of 1825:* The first treaty of Prairie du Chien was signed by William Clark and Lewis Cass for the United States and representatives of the Anishinaabeg/Chippewa, Sioux, Sac and Fox, Menominee, Ioway, Winnebago, Council of the Three Fires of Chippewa, Ottawa and Potawatomi on August 19, 1825 and proclaimed on February 6, 1826. Due to the overall tribal movements toward the western direction under pressure of encroaching settlers, the Sioux Nation resisted and came into conflict with other tribes moving west into their traditional territory. The United States negotiated the treaty to try to reduce inter-tribal warfare. The treaty begins by establishing peace between the Sioux and their neighbors: Chippewa, Sac and Fox, and Iowa peoples. The treaty continues by demarcating formal boundaries among each of the tribal groups, often called the "Prairie du Chien Line." For peoples accustomed to ranging over a wide area, the Prairie du Chien Line served as a hindrance, as it provided that tribes were to hunt only within their acknowledged limits. Due to the vast scope of the *Treaty of Prairie du Chien* and the fact that not all of the necessary tribes had representatives at its signing, the treaty provided for additional councils to be held the following year in 1826.

A new county, with the name of Chippewa, was created by the same authority in 1825. This county was formed of territory taken from the northern part of Michilimackinac, and extended along the entire southern shore of Lake Superior.

The "Population of La Pointe reaches high water mark of 2,500 souls, traders, voyageurs, half-breeds and Indian peoples."

1830: Frederik Ayer, who became friends with arrives from Mackinac to begin a school named the "Warrens School." The Protestant mission was founded on Madelaine Island by Frederick Ayer.

August 30, 1831: Reverend Sherman Hall, a Presbyterian, arrives to start a mission and school that Lyman Warren had advocated for. Hall, wife and interpreter, Mrs. John Campbell stay at Warren's residence.

1832: There were 185 Ojibway of pure native stock (72 adults, 113 children) settled on Madeline Island according to Henry Rowe School craft. . Religious affiliations of mixed bloods, called "Bois Brule's' ", were predominantly Catholic.

August 20, 1833: A meeting was held to organize the first Protestant church in Wisconsin. Attendants to the confession of faith and convenient were Rev. W.T. Boutwell, Rev. Sherman Hall, Mrs. Betsey Parker-Hall, Lyman M. Warren, Edmund Ely, Charles W. Borup, John Campbell, Mrs. E. Campbell, Mr. Frederik Ayer, & Misses Delia Cook, Josette Pyant, Sabrina Stevens.

John Jacob Astor & Ramsey Crooks form a general purchase agreement for American Fur Company.

1834: Ramsay Crooks heads a group of investors and purchases American Fur Company from John Jacob Astor and continued to operate the business under this name. Crooks also initiated a fishing operation on Lake Superior and moved the company's headquarters from Mackinac to La Pointe. The old trading post had long been inadequate and in early 1835, the company began building a new post on the West side of Madeline Island.

Father Frederik Baraga founded the first Catholic mission at La Pointe and constructed the Old Mission Church. The mission hall work starts and is completed in January or February, 1835.

January 1, 1835: John Jacob Astor retained his stock in American Fur Company through 1834, sold, and on this date Ramsey Crooks and associates assumed formal ownership. Lyman Warren owned 10 shares of the 1000 available stock.

Spring and summer: In a small and experimental way American Fur Company, as a possible hedge against the eventual exhaustion of furs, conducted trial commercial fishing trial run ventures at La Pointe, Grand Marais and Isle Royale.

John Jacob Astor's American Fur Company diversifies it fur trade business to commercial fishing. AFC establishes a fishing station at La Pointe and equipped its residents with seine nets, wooden barrels and salt. By 1837, the LaPointe Indians provided the company with 2000 barrels of salted fish per year. Ojibwa women found paid work in the fishery also, cleaning and packing fish. *Here begins the advent of the commercial fishing industry in Chequamegon Bay.*

July 27, 1835: Father Irenaeus Frederic Baraga arrives.

Lyman Warren, Charles Oakes and Charles William Wulf Borup move the old La Pointe village from the south end of the island to its present "New Fort" location, a 400 foot dock with a fish house mounted on the end, 150 longer than present day (1957) was built. Hamilton Nelson Ross

Reverend Sherman Hall establishes first Protestant mission at "Middle Port", halfway between the village and old fort on Southeast corner of La Pointe. The island population is about 600.

1836: "The Territory of Wisconsin was an organized territory of the United States that existed from July 3, 1836, until May 29, 1848, when an eastern portion of the territory was admitted to the Union as the State of Wisconsin. The area that would later be part of the second—and by far the longest lasting—incarnation of the Wisconsin Territory was originally part of the Northwest Territory. At that time the Wisconsin Territory was split off from Michigan Territory in 1836 as the state of Michigan prepared for statehood. However, the *original* Wisconsin Territory, as established by statute on April 20, 1836, did *not* just include land from the original Northwest Territory. In 1833, Congress had annexed huge tracts of land west of the Mississippi to the then Michigan Territory. When the Wisconsin Territory was split off from the Michigan Territory, it inherited this western land. Thus, the 1836 Wisconsin Territory included all of the present-day states of Minnesota, Wisconsin, and Iowa and that part of the Dakotas that lay east of the Missouri River. The Territory east of the Mississippi River had originally been part of the Northwest Territory, which had itself been included in the secession by Britain in 1783. Most of the remaining land of the original Wisconsin Territory was originally part of the Louisiana Purchase, though a small fraction was part of a parcel ceded by Great Britain in 1818. This land west of the Mississippi had been split off from the Missouri in 1821 and attached to the Michigan Territory in 1834. In 1838, the Iowa Territory was formed, reducing the Wisconsin Territory to the boundaries for the next ten years;

upon granting statehood to Wisconsin, its boundaries were once again reduced, to their present location."

The *Territory of Wisconsin* was organized April 20, by act of Congress. Henry Dodge was appointed governor and on July 4, with John S. Horner of Virginia as secretary and Charles Dunn, David Irvin, and William C. Frazier as Supreme Court justices. The new officers were sworn in at Mineral Point, then the largest town in the Territory. The first territorial assembly met at Old Belmont, October 25.

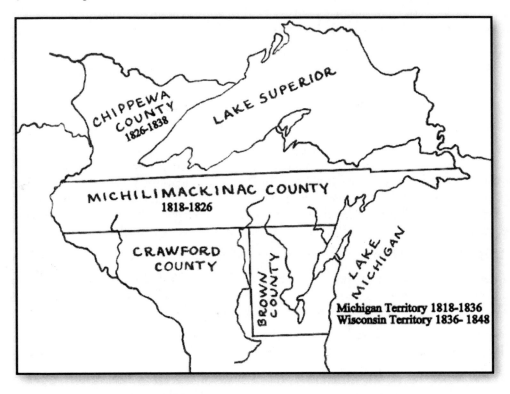

Territory of Wisconsin 1836-1848 with Counties: 1836
BHA Pike Research Center Archive Collection

July 8, 1837: "Sacred to the Memory of Michel Cadotte, who departed this life-Aged 72, 11 Months, 16 days. Cadotte made large profits in the fur trade, but died relatively poor due to the generosity of his nature toward indignant natives.

July 29: The United States entered into a treaty with several bands of Ojibway Indians. Under the terms of the treaty, the native people – Anishinaabeg, ceded the northern third of present-day Wisconsin and more than 3,000,000 acres of land between the St. Croix and Mississippi rivers. The United States, in turn, guaranteed to respect certain hunting, fishing and gathering rights on ceded territories and make annuity payments for the next 20 years.

1838-1840: Chequamegon area civil governance is under Crawford County.

1838: A large expansion in the fish business at La Pointe started and to which were shipped out 4000 barrels of product. Coopers were kept busy all winter in anticipation of the next years business.

1839: Charles Borup wrote to Ramsay Crooks (American Fur Company) about plans for a new fishing outpost in the Apostle Islands. But the company found it difficult to market the fish in a depressed economy. In 1841 American Fur Company ended its commercial fishing operations.

5000 barrels were shipped by early October to allow for transportation to the Sault, the main street portage of that city, and reload on Lake Huron for destiny markets. The American Fur Company, a newly formed partnership, ordered 2600 barrels of salt in anticipation of the 1840 fish season from Moses Burnett of Syracuse, New York for the Northern (La Pointe) Outfit.

Ojibwa "Battle of the Brule." Chief Buffalo's war strategy of sending flanking forces to the West of the Brule ensured Chippewa victory for Chief Hole-in-the-Bay, head of Lake Superior Chippewa against the Sioux on the banks of the Brule River.

1840-1845: Chequamegon area civil governance is under St. Croix County.

1840: The first Protestant church in the Chequamegon area is completed at LaPointe. Reverend Sherman Hall's translation of the New Testament into Ojibwa was completed.

1841: Douglass Houghton, a geologist surveying the Chequamegon Bay area this year noted the rich, red sandstone outcroppings and commented on their potential value.

Father Baraga counters the Protestant church building scenario as the Catholic faithful constructed a larger church on the same site as the present church. It was 50 long by 30 wide; with a beautiful alter with a picture of St. Joseph painted in 1834 by a skilled artist named Lang, of Laibach.

1842: The Copper Treaty of 1842.: An agreement was negotiated October 4, at LaPointe, Wisconsin, Madeline Island, with the Ojibwa, who ceded all their remaining lands in Wisconsin and Michigan; Ojibwa leaders, however, protested that in this and the 1837 Treaty they had only given the U.S. rights to use the products of the land and had never ceded ownership. In September the Ojibwa people signed the "Copper Treaty", where-by their lands on the southwestern shore of Lake Superior were ceded.

Copper is discovered in Upper Michigan and by 1848 iron ore was located in the Gogebic and Penokee Ranges but mining was delayed until the 1880 because of transportation logistics.

1844: Merchant Julius Austrian moves to La Pointe and begins to purchase thousands of acres of land, including the present site where La Pointe is located.

1845-1860: Chequamegon area civil governance is under La Pointe County. La Pointe is the county seat.

1845: LaPointe County, including in its area the present counties of Douglas, Bayfield and Ashland, was set off from St. Croix County. La Pointe County is organized, with the village of La Pointe as the county seat.

The propeller *Independence*, 105 feet long, and with a capacity of 262 tons, became the first steamer on Lake Superior. It took seven weeks to portage the ship on rollers around the rapids at Sault Saint Marie. The *Independence* stopped at LaPointe, where, according to one crew member, "we gave a dreadful scare with the appearance of our craft, and the noise of the steam whistle."

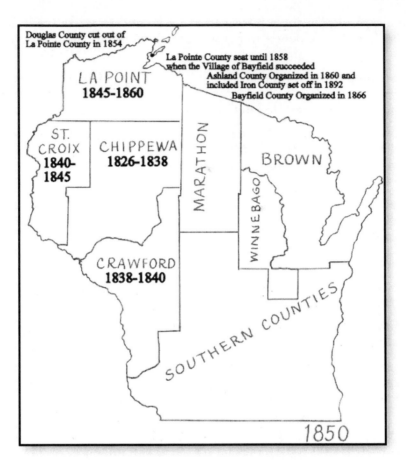

Douglas County cut out of
La Pointe County in 1854

La Pointe County seat until 1858
when the Village of Bayfield succeeded

Ashland County Organized in 1860 and
included Iron County set off in 1892

Bayfield County Organized in 1866

LA POINT
1845-1860

ST. CROIX
1840-1845

CHIPPEWA
1826-1838

MARATHON

BROWN

WINNEBAGO

CRAWFORD
1838-1840

SOUTHERN COUNTIES

1850

Wisconsin Territory County's: 1836-1848
BHA Pike Research Center Archive Collection

1846: The people of Wisconsin voted in favor of a State government. Congress passed the enabling act, and the first constitutional convention opened at Madison, October 15.

1847: Henry Mower Rice enters the Bayfield and Chequamegon Bay area, most likely traveling on the Bayfield-St. Croix Road or by steamer from Superior City, Wisconsin, when he arrived to La Pointe in 1847 as a federal Indian commissioner trying to convince the Ojibwa to move to the west of the Mississippi River.

April 5, 1847: The first Wisconsin Constitution was rejected by popular vote. The second constitutional convention opened at Madison, December 15.

May 29, 1848: Under Act of Congress Wisconsin is admitted to the Union as the 30th State. Nelson Dewey was elected first State governor. The first legislature convened June 5, and two days later the State officers were sworn in. Henry Dodge and Isaac P. Walker were elected United States senators, and Andrew G. Miller appointed judge of United States district court. A free school system was established by law. A land grant for a university was made by Congress and the State University was incorporated.

(Several opinions about the origin of the word Wisconsin exist. Louis Kellogg, who was an authority on Wisconsin history, suggests that the State derived its name from the principal river which runs centrally through it. An Ojibwa term, Weeskonsan signifies the gathering of the waters on account of its numbers of branches near its head waters concentrated into one stream)

During the prospecting activity of the Gogebic & Penokee Ranges in this year, the "Ontonagon Boulder" was discovered. Reduced in weight from the day of Alexander Henry (1790s') the pure copper piece weighed near 3000 lbs and was placed in the Smithsonian Institution of Washington.

Minnesota Territory & State of Wisconsin
BHA Pike Research Center Archive Collection

1850: La Pointe is the only port in the western portion of Lake Superior. The 1850 federal census counted a population of 463 in the village of La Pointe.

1852: U.S. General Land Surveyors arrive in the Chequamegon region to survey and divide ceded Ojibwe lands into Townships and sections, a prerequisite for federal sale of these lands.

Congress authorizes the construction of a canal and lock system at Sault Saint Marie, Michigan.

1853: A group of investors led by Senator Stephen A. Douglas of Illinois founded Superior City [Superior, Wisconsin] at the lake's most western point.

September 29, 1854: Great Ojibwa Chief Buffalo, Chief of all Lake Superior Chippewa, signs *Treaty of 1854*. Ojibwa peoples are not to be expatriated to Minnesota. Homeland reservations with federally allocated rights to hunt, fish and gather are created. The Bad River and Red Cliff Bands of Lake Superior Chippewa reservations are established.

October 9, 1854: Henry M. Rice files for a portion of land located in the proximity of Bayfield city proper, and spearheads a speculative venture in Bayfield area.

Bayfield resident, Asaph Whittlesey and his family settle at the head of Chequamegon Bay. In 1855 Frederick Prentice platted a town called Bay City a few miles away. The settlement was slow to grow, and by the Civil War only one family remained. People began to return to the site in 1870 and in 1872 the two sites were merged into the town of Ashland.

1855: Completion of the Sault locks in 1855 opens the water route to the great lakes and east coast. No longer would fish, lumber and staples carrying vessels need be carted around the Falls of St. Mary.

Bayfield Townsite Company in the works: Robinson Derling Pike, one of Bayfield's captains of industry recalls, "I remember very well being at the office at La Pointe with father, (Elijah Pike) I was a mere lad of 17, and I recollect hearing them discuss with Julius Austrian the question of running the streets in Bayfield north and south and the avenues east and west, or whether they should run diagonally due to the topography of the property. Mr. Austrian decided on the plan as the town is now laid out."

Nazaire La Bonte was speaking at the 50 anniversary of Bayfield when he mentioned the Harbor City was set out as a speculative venture. In this year Rice acquired a patent for 349 Acres of land. The Bayfield Land Company consisted of Henry Mower Rice-President, John D. Livingston, Rittenhouse, Davidson and Payne."

March 21, 1855: Henry M. Rice obtained land patent for 320 Acres presently the city of Bayfield, signed by President Franklin Pierce.

April 3, 1855: Henry M. Rice gives Mr. William McAboy the power of attorney, "in his name and stead, to survey, lie out and apply into blocks, squares, avenues, streets and alleys" that part of Bayfield.

November 17, 1855: Eliza Pike, wife (Elizabeth Kimmey) son Robinson Derling, & daughter Adeline arrive at Pikes Bay in the fall of 1855. Pike received land patent Number 101 for 120 Acres of land in Section 28, Township 50, Range 4 West.

October 1855: In a letter to Bayfield citizens at the 50 anniversary of Bayfield R. D. Pike states, "We arrived at La Pointe in the early part of October, 1855. We remained at La Pointe for 5-10 days and then went to Pike's bay with all our supplies, oxen and cow on what was known as Uncle Robert Morrin's bateau. Uncle Robert and William Morrin were present when the first trees were cut.

March 24, 1856: Founding of Bayfield, Wisconsin; On the morning of the 24th of March, inhabitants of La Pointe were startled to see smoke curling up through the trees on the thickly covered shore. Thinking that a band of Indians had come over land and were camped here, a few men came over and found a party of nine men under the charge of John C. Hanley, who had driven down on the ice from Superior and landed on the point where Mr. Currie G. Bell's house now stands (Lot 11, Block 88) and it was where the first trees were cut. The first cabin built was nearly opposite Mr. Bell's residence, and where the old land office sat.

End of Volume One

About the Author

Robert J. Nelson

First, let it be known, that a professionally trained, bona-fide graduate of a University history department, and, a "credentialed" historian I am not. I am, as I describe myself, merely a "history detective", "amateur" at best who finds probing around in old newspapers for long forgotten stories and discovering old photos that match the tale, a simply irresistible hobby. Second, I am Bayfield born, raised, of Scandinavian Teutonic stock, retired and remain so in Bayfield Township. Devoting time to Board membership duties at *Bayfield Heritage Association-Inc.*, *Apostle Islands Historic Preservation Conservancy*, some speaking engagements and spending time at Rocky Island, the Nelson family's historic fish camp in the Apostle Islands fixing and fishing fills in the daily log book. Conserving and enhancing Wisconsin' natural resources, teaching and training young adults for the world of work and continued education, in the now non-operational, Wisconsin Conservation Corps near to twenty years and serving the School District of Bayfield students as board president and member for near nine years are my proudest accomplishments.

Published books include *Apostle Islanders; the People and Culture*- 2008; *Skal Vi Ga Hjem: John and Andrea Nelson Norwegian Immigrant to America*- 2010; *To America Frank Muhlke-Thyra Jensen German and Danish Baltic Sea Immigrants*- 2010 and *Memories and Minutes; A History of School District Number One, Township of Bayfield*- 2008.My work related to facilitating publishing of Bayfield's wonderful historian and old family and my friend Eleanor Knight and her work that fills the chapters of, *Tales of Bayfield Pioneers; A History of Bayfield*- 2008 is a highlight of my endeavors.

Index of Photos

Index of Names & Businesses